50

BUSINESSES
TO START
FROM HOME

50
BUSINESSES
TO START
FROM HOME

MEL LEWIS

PIATKUS

© 1994 Mel Lewis

First published in 1994 by
July Piatkus (Publishers) Ltd
5 Windmill Street, London W1P 1HF

The moral right of the author has been asserted

*A catalogue record for this book is available
from the British Library*

ISBN 0-7499-1322-3

Edited by Carol Franklin
Designed by Chris Warner

Set in Concorde, Melior and Rockwell by
Computerset, Harmondsworth
Printed & bound in Great Britain by
Biddles Ltd, Guildford & King's Lynn

Contents

GENERAL

Introduction

All business starts with a sale, and working from home is a beguilingly easy sale to make.

According to author Fay Weldon – who writes by hand, where the mood takes her, often at the kitchen table – 'Mornings are best . . . nearer your dreams . . . The minute you get dressed you've had it.'

Illustrator Maurice Sendak gets dressed at 11.30 a.m. but refuses to start work until 2.30 in the afternoon, though with equal regularity he will carry on working after midnight.

You can do that kind of thing at home. And many more people are doing it; some 700,000 (two-thirds of them women), according to The Labour Force Survey (Department of Employment, Autumn 93), double that number if you talk to managing editor of *Home Business* magazine Mike Beardall.

Clearly homeworkers have lots going for them. They have no need for expensive 'power dressing'; they can don T-shirt and jeans or whatever suits their mood and the demands of the day. While Londoners are reputed to spend an average six weeks a year commuting, work from home and you can generally make it to the kitchen table, or desk, in about two minutes flat. Not surprisingly, homeworkers spend more time working, enjoy their tasks more and also have more quality time left over to share with their families.

Working from home gives you the freedom to achieve your goals in your own time, in your own way, according to your own natural body rhythms. You're also totally free to fail, of course, and the easy temptations of an unstructured life claim many victims.

For, contrary to common belief, working for yourself is no escape from management, merely a change of boss. Suddenly you start working under the most sympathetic or the most chaotic manager of all – you!

Again, the choice is yours. Every day needs to be created from scratch, generally without help. Succeeding with a home-run business is the ultimate challenge, the greatest satisfaction and an awesome responsibility, if others depend on your consistent and sustained earning power.

Talking of money, please note that this book is not about writing business plans, raising capital, understanding tax or VAT, except at crucial points under specific topics. Instead, you should look on these chapters as windows on to good ideas.

Thanks to technology a 'cottage industry' no longer means macramé or jam making: computers, faxes and electronic mail enable anyone to keep close tabs on clients, colleagues and suppliers – even from a kitchen table. The new technology-based occupations are represented in some depth, probably for the first time in a book of this type. And so too is the burgeoning area of consultancy; just the job for the flexibly employed who still enjoy notional corporate office space, are in retained employment, or who have recently retired from 'driving a big desk'.

As you will now discover, my purpose in writing this book is quite immodest and dangerously ambitious. Anyone can inform; the intention here is to intrigue and inspire. The best home businesses (all businesses?) thrive on enthusiasm, and that, as you may already know, is the greatest energy source in the world and your best talisman for success.

Mel Lewis
The Waveney Valley
Suffolk

In the Beginning

WHAT KIND OF BUSINESS IS RIGHT FOR YOU?

Knowing yourself and what you enjoy doing is the key to succeeding with a home business. Research yourself properly, and you are far more likely to walk the line between happy enterprise and belly-up failure without stumbling.

This book is less concerned with how to become a grim success story in business, and much more with how to carve out a rewarding and humane lifestyle, avoiding the inimical and irrelevant pressures of commuting and office politics.

The swing is towards quality, personal service and products with individual appeal. Working from home is the modern way to 'deliver the goods' on every count.

Working from home also gives you more time in which to work, and a more comfortable and usually more stylish workplace. I can never understand how people spend up to a third of their lives in offices, putting up with sad colours, second-rate seating and lighting that would distress a tadpole. At home you can truly be yourself. Not only will your work improve, but so will the other two-thirds of your life.

SELF-ASSESSMENT

How do you assess your aptitudes, talents and skills? Possibly your favourite leisure time activities have led you to wondering, 'Could I make money at this?' The answer doesn't come easily. You'll need to take detailed stock on every level. Do

3

you enjoy being alone, working in a studious, quiet way or do you prefer being with people? And this begs the question, do people enjoy being with you? What are the commercial possibilities of pursuing a hobby professionally?

Another route to self-discovery is to refer to books like *Marketing Yourself* and *The Perfect CV* (both published in 1991 by Piatkus Books). You're not looking for a job; on the contrary, the aim is to avoid regular, stultifying pay-as-you-earn employment, with artificial constraints on your earning power, and little heed of your own work rhythms and creative needs.

You should ignore the job-targeting aspect of these books, and instead focus on the chapters that tell you how to list and analyse your potential. This could help you find direction and shape your new, independent life.

Look at some examples. David was training to be a draughtsman. He liked the job but viewed his promotion prospects with dismay. It was, he realised, a matter of 'waiting for dead colleagues' shoes'. He was about to get married, to a hairdresser, and was hungry for income. He was good with his hands and had creative flair. Why not try hairdressing himself? Starting out as a home hairdresser, he went on to become an award-winning stylist.

Jackie, a mother with two children, longed to run a playgroup from home, but found the council regulations unrealistically demanding. Being a bit theatrical and outgoing, she decided to try a musical playgroup, operating from church and community halls, rather than home. She now works five days a week, with a friend, and both enjoy a better than average income.

Where most playgroups go on hold in the school holidays, this one continues to thrive, as mums with holidaying schoolchildren relish the break the group gives them.

Not every attribute or skill you may have can transfer usefully to a home-based occupation. For instance, take the ability to make friends easily, or being able to engage a total stranger in conversation. You'd think this might open a window on to journalism ... or market research. However, some people find writing for a living is a lonely and an intense activity – the greater part of writing, one wit said, is applying the seat of one's pants to the seat of the chair!

And market research may not suit those who don't boast a hearty constitution. A lot of the work involves traipsing round streets and knocking on strangers' doors, in search of respondents. Even a 'good talker' may dry up when faced with a spate of rejections from people too busy to give up their precious time, or unsympathetic to products or surveys.

You may need to try out a number of options before you find the one that suits you best. The beauty of working for yourself, from home, is that you can easily make choices and change your business. You are no longer bound by what jobs happen to be available locally or who you can manage to impress in an interview.

EQUIPPING YOUR HOME BUSINESS OFFICE

Almost every home business needs some kind of office to enable you to handle essential paperwork – sending letters or bills to clients, ordering stock, sorting tax or VAT matters, and so on. This doesn't have to be a room that's used exclusively as an office (in fact, for tax and planning reasons, it may well be better not to have a room that's only used for business purposes), but you do need your own work 'territory', an area that is not regularly invaded by the family or others looking for a place to work, play or eat.

If you try to reserve the kitchen table as your desk, one thing is guaranteed: kitchen sink drama! Your own room, or work area, provides three key elements that are vital to the efficient running of your business.

■ **Security**   You must be sure that things stay where they are put, and that you can impose your own work routines and work rhythms within this space, and preferably also decorate and furnish according to your own tastes.

■ **Privacy** Concentration is a fickle state of mind, and being at the mercy of interruptions, or distractions, such as music not of your choosing or television, will quickly wrench you out of that state of grace.

Having your own private space eliminates other problems, too, such as when you need to talk to people in a confidential way. It takes years to develop a friendly, businesslike and effective telephone manner – and one second to lose it if you have to 'perform' in front of others who share your work area.

■ **Organisation** The last thing you want to have to do is clear up after a work session. Contrary to what mums, dads and teachers tell us, a tidy desk does not always mirror a tidy mind. Lose the thread of work in progress, because papers have been 'straightened', and it could cost dear in lost time and frustration found.

Desks

Most desks seem to have been designed in the PC – pre-computer – era. By the time you've arranged your computer, printer, phone, fax, desklight, pen pot, notepad and Filofax you're fresh out of desk space.

One simple answer is to use two tables, arranged in an L-shape. The biggest item you will need to set up is your computer. Either get this up and off the desk, on a cantilever type of stand that clips on to the back of the desk or invest in a computer 'workstation' (on lockable castors). The keyboard slots under the monitor, and there's usually a tier for printer and a ledge for a mousepad. Clip-on lecterns can hold reference papers at eye height.

Chairs

The best office chairs are upholstered in leather, have rising seats, adjustable back squabs and cost a mint. You could buy a very good antique chair for the same price and thereby own an appreciating, rather than a depreciating, asset. Insist on a chair with a good back support and arms. I read somewhere that a chair with arms is five times as comfortable as one without arms! Don't arms get in the way of typing? Not on my *c.*1860 yew and elm captain's chair they don't. The arms curve graciously outwards.

Filing

There is no such thing as the perfect filing system. The main requirement is not to misplace paperwork. Since few activities generate as much reference material and paper as writing for a living, the following personal solutions may be useful to you.

I throw everything relating to a particular assignment into a bright-coloured plastic box the size of a kitchen sink. Even without a lid, the boxes stack. These storage boxes can be bought, in various sizes, at hardware stores or much more cheaply, I discovered, at Toys 'Я' Us.

Every wadge of paper in the box is placed in a clear plastic wallet, 'stepped, thumb cut, and open two sides', according to the packaging. Coloured wallets are a waste of time; you can't read what's inside. I buy wallets by the hundred at a discount stationery shop and save at least 50 per cent on high street prices.

When any particular project is complete it needs to be stored. I return all the books to their shelves and file the papers, labelled on the front, in much larger zip-up clear plastic, dust-proof wallets, so again, you can read what's inside without opening them up.

If the material needs to remain active I put it in Esselte files, obtainable from Ryman or other stationery shops. These look like a rigid plastic version of the traditional cardboard box file, and stand sturdily on their narrow ends.

Unless your office is the second smallest room in the house, the greatest filing area you own is in fact the floor. The floor by the door is the perfect prompt to a busy home worker likely to rush out of the house forgetting things. If you don't believe this, count how many people bring you the material you've left by the door with a comment such as 'I found this by the door ...' – proof positive that the system works!

Computers and other equipment

Few businesses operate without paper and, regardless of the trumpetings of the infant computer industry, computers do not eliminate paper. On the contrary, they churn the stuff out and create paper mountains. Nevertheless, you'll find it hard to live without one. But which one?

It's easy to get swept along with computer hype. Computer companies grow rich on consumers' fear of being 'left behind'. Are you sure a comfortable old-tech computer and printer aren't adequate for your own business? They may even be preferable.

For example, immaculately laser-printed correspondence, especially when the text is 'justified' – squared up either side, like the printed page of a book – lacks the familiar spontaneity of an electric typewriter or a 'slow' daisywheel printer.

The trick is to question everything. Do you need a 'laptop' computer whose 'footprint' is no larger than an A4 size piece of paper, still less a 'palmtop' that sits in the hand?

According to *The Times*, 'The portable computer you buy now will be out of date in six months as cheaper and more powerful models come along.' They will also be more versatile, with a built-in fax, cellular phone, photocopier and trouser press, too, probably ...

Small is usually more expensive in the computer world and small may also be less user-friendly. Fast keyboard operators (especially those who dropped out of the touch-typing course) could find the squashed-up keyboard of a laptop hard to use without tripping over other, unwanted keys.

Correcting mistakes wastes valuable time and stems the flow of words or figures. You are less likely to suffer that problem with a proper desktop computer with discrete console and generously architectured, separate keyboard.

One important thing that must be said in favour of laptops, other than their obvious benefits for working while you are travelling and taking up less space on a crowded desk, relates to safety.

The typical laptop has a liquid crystal display, just like calculators and digital watches. Tiny crystals, held in a viscous suspension, are illuminated from behind. So, unlike the TV or VDU screen of a desktop monitor, which emits very small amounts of radiation, worrying some scientists and doctors, the screen of a laptop is perfectly safe.

Software advances force the pace of change, much of it sensible and practical. Why learn weird letter codes when your 'mouse' can click an arrow against an icon image showing a printer, a disk, filing cabinet or trash can? Before choosing a computer or software, spend time with the two main contenders to see which you prefer: Apple and IBM, and the latter's bevy of compatible clones.

Working with a new computer is like buying a new pair of shoes. You can probably break them in, but your feet may suffer first. Yet the shoes you enjoy wearing the most are the ones that were comfortable from day one. With computer software and hardware it's the brain that can be tormented.

A piece of good advice is to use makers' handbooks only as a last resort and instead buy books on your software written by independent authors. Or ask a friend or colleague with computer experience, 'How do you do that?' – whatever it is you want your computer to do.

How hi tech equipped do you need to be? All of the gadgetry comes down in price with market demand and competitive selling. Be aware of what is available and how it might help your business, but remember that nothing is worth buying for its own sake.

A **modem** is a device that enables you to send and receive information via your computer, using the normal phone lines. A **fax machine** enables you to send and receive printed information via the phone.

The original and most common type of fax machine uses a coated paper that yields what looks like a very indifferent quality photocopy. Worse, the image fades in hours if exposed to direct sunlight and sometimes in a matter of months, even in a file kept in a drawer.

The trend is towards 'plain paper' fax machines that overcome this problem. But the technology is young and the price not yet right.

Photocopiers are rightly low down on any home business shopping list, being, historically at least, big and dirty. And wasn't there always the risk of getting locked into some horrific rental or leasing contract that would end up costing more than the mortgage? Most of these anxieties have been alleviated by the trade.

Because, as it seems to me, there is a connection between the size of a copier and the quality of its copies, it still makes sense to buy the service from a shop with a big professional copier, rather than own or rent a smaller machine. Instead of paying up to 12p a page, I have come to an agreement with a local estate agent. My cash for photocopies helps him fund the machine; he charges me less than half the going rate.

HOW TO PROMOTE YOUR BUSINESS OR SERVICE

Ironically, the very strengths of working from home are also a major weakness: nobody knows you're there! Shops and offices usually have some kind of street presence, and therefore benefit from passing trade. You probably don't. Marketing is your passport to success.

'Marketing' is a term often used as a synonym for 'sell'. There's more to it than that. 'More properly', according to *Biz-speak, A Dictionary of Business Terms, Slang and Jargon* (by Rachel S. Epstein and Nina Liebman, published by Harrap, 1987), '[it] means to produce, distribute, and promote a product or service after studying how and where buyers are likely to respond.' 'Study' is the key word here.

Avoid the desire to be 'creative' and original. Never worry about using tried and tested marketing strategies. You can decide to 'do your own thing' and learn from your own experiences, but you'll get on faster, less painfully and more cheaply, if you learn from the experiences of others. Your aim is not to sidestep traditional marketing methods, but to use them all – tweaked for greater impact.

Door-to-door mailings

If you needed a light for your cigarette or wanted to know the time of day, you'd turn to the person standing next to you, or knock on a neighbour's door, right? So surely it makes sense to seek trade first of all with those who live within easy reach?

Amazingly, this truism seems to go over the heads of many otherwise clued-up businesspeople, homeworkers and shopkeepers, who overlook door-to-door leafleting as an essential and obvious first step towards impacting the marketplace.

The cheapest leaflets – also called flyers or mailers – are flat pieces of paper printed on one side. A normal A4 letterhead size gives room for copy and illustration. If your message is short, half that size, A5, may be big enough.

You can write and design leaflets yourself, but the results from the work of a professional copywriter and designer will leave your own efforts standing. Professional design and artwork, the 'fair copy' from which the printer works, will cost slightly more than copywriting.

Find a home-based designer who will keep your designs and text on disk, so your follow-up leaflets will be cheaper.

Jobbing printers have their tongues hanging out for work and will probably print 500 leaflets in black ink on white paper reasonably cheaply. Curiously, the more you have printed, the cheaper it gets. There is no VAT on leaflets and it is always worth trying to knock printers (or any trader) down on price.

What should your leaflet say? Be brief and focus on the benefits you offer. For example:

11

Retired master shoe-maker at your service

SHOES NEED MENDING?

Why pay high street prices for shoe repairs?

My prices are at least 30% lower.

But my work is 50% higher on quality!

First-class repairs in leather or man-made materials.

Ladies' gents' children's shoes welcomed.

Trainers? No problem!

Fast service guaranteed.

*Call any weekday between 9 a.m. and 5 p.m.
or phone ....*

The address is clearly printed at the bottom, with a miniature map if needed. This isn't the place for a treatise on copywriting, though there is more in the section on copywriting on page 30, but I'll say this. A Yale University survey discovered the 12 words below to be the most persuasive words in the world:

YOU	NEW	HEALTH	DISCOVER
MONEY	RESULTS	SAFETY	PROVEN
SAVE	EASY	LOVE	GUARANTEE

The more of those words, those notions, you can sensibly weave into your publicity material the better.

How should you distribute your leaflet? *Yellow Pages* list firms that specialise in this, but you might find a cheaper source closer to home, for example your newsagent or milkman might co-operate. Inserting 2,500 leaflets into my local freesheet cost just £30. If the job's done privately, on foot door-to-door, employ someone you can trust: I've seen a lot of publicity material on the floors of empty shops and derelict houses.

Shop window cards

Who would have thought you could run a business or shift hundreds of pounds' worth of goods through a few words on a postcard in a shop window? But it's true. I'm trying out the following card to help make extra money out of expensively bought wordprocessing equipment:

**COULD A NEW CV GET YOU
A BETTER JOB?**

Is your CV old-fashioned . . . too long?
Modern managers warm to candidates who 'cut the cackle'. I'll focus your career . . . help you get the job interviews you want. Work with Mel Lewis, business books author and self-promotion expert.

CVs from £10.

Tel: ....

Cards should always be typed, never hand-written. If you're selling goods a small colour photo works wonders, as does any kind of design, coloured border or highlighted text. It makes your card yell to passers-by, 'Read me first'.

Business cards

Do business cards matter? When you next find yourself in a group of businesspeople exchanging cards, and you're the one whose cards are being 'reprinted', come back and tell me

13

whether that mattered or not. Business cards are good for business, it's as simple as that.

Any neat, black-on-white printed card is better than none. But since you never get a second chance to make a first impression, doesn't it make sense to make yours a bit special? I don't mean flashy, but different, maybe even useful . . .

Cards should have printing that is big enough for poor eyesight. Then you should spell out what you do:

John Jones

NETWORK MARKETING CONSULTANT

Emily Nader

CURTAINS AND SOFT FURNISHINGS MADE TO MEASURE

Stick to standard sized cards; they're more likely to find a permanent home in a wallet or purse, or slip comfortably into those handy see-through plastic business card holders many people own.

How else can you ensure your card stays around? Give added value, as with the leaflet. Print useful information on the back, perhaps something that relates to your business . . . metric conversion figures . . . or even a mirrored back! I've never seen the latter done. But why not?

Letterheads

Letterheads are a study in themselves. I must have been one of the first people in the UK to put a photograph of myself on my headed paper, though it's common enough in America. Too flash? I find it very useful.

When I phone to chase business letters my name has often gone out of the head of the person who read my letter. But when I mention the picture, all is clarity and light!

Avoid slick-looking images, the full zoot suit or costume treatment. Everyone knows you've got smart outfits in your wardrobe and won't turn up to a business meeting in mufti. Search instead for a friendly-looking image. I found a crisp holiday snap where I was holding my eight-year-old son's hand, and looking fit, tanned and relaxed. I decided to print the whole picture. Underneath the caption reads: 'Mel Lewis & Son'.

Local newspaper advertising

Advertising and copywriting are crafts in themselves, as you surely appreciate. Advertising isn't cheap, and it isn't the blank space that will win you business, it's what you do with it. Therefore don't do it amateurishly yourself; get a professional wordsmith and designer to do the job properly.

Advertising professionals are struggling as much as anyone these days, and you will not need to pay a fortune, or even the asking price ... The newspaper will probably offer to throw in copywriting, photography and design just to encourage you to take the ad space. Pass up the offer. You get what you pay for in this life.

What you should deal on, though, is a good position in the paper, generally thought to be high on a right-hand page, and a bargain deal. If you cannot get the paper to drop the price, insist that they up the size of the space your money buys, as this is a very cheap option for any advertising manager.

The offer of free 'advertorial', limp advertising puffery masquerading as genuine, unbiased editorial, should be shunned – unless you have the option of writing the material yourself. If so, go back to your pro copywriter, and get the message and angles right.

Bookkeeping for beginners

It will pay you to be optimistic when it comes to keeping accounts. Assume you will need to show figures to the tax inspectors and eventually also to the Customs & Excise (who administer VAT).

Do you need an accountant? Think like a professional and you will grow like one. Part of that credo is that you use good, personally recommended people.

I've heard tales of people struggling to get a response or sympathy from the Inland Revenue and it makes me weep. Accountants know how to talk to these people, and there's no doubt tax officers prefer to talk to their colleagues on the other side of the fence, rather than members of the public. Besides, accountants know wrinkles it will take you a lifetime to learn.

It is essential to keep records, bills, receipts, paperwork, invoices and related correspondence. I use the large plastic box filing system mentioned earlier. All bills go in the box and are sorted every three months into the following categories.

- **Output**, what I earn, grouped under clients and broken down with columns for gross figure, net figure and VAT element (gross less net). The VAT part is what I owe HM Customs & Excise.
- **Input**, my expenses broken down into fuel (petrol, diesel; I claim 90 per cent of my total fuel bills, the maximum generally allowed), motor maintenance, phone bill, stationery, printing, photocopiers, photography, design, advertising, secretarial/research and miscellaneous.

The gross, net and VAT element columns apply here too. The VAT element is what HM Customs & Excise 'owes me'. I subtract the expenses/INPUT VAT from the income/OUTPUT VAT and send in a cheque every quarter.

If the period was a bad trading one, or few people happened to have been billed in those three months, and you have spent more than you earned, you may find yourself claiming money, not paying it out.

PLANNING PERMISSION, BUILDING REGULATIONS, BUSINESS RATES AND OTHER BUSYBODIES

Local authorities are empowered to be far more intrusive than is generally realised. Strictly speaking permission needs to be sought to install a wash handbasin in a bedroom or store items other than a car in a garage. Of course you can keep your garden tools in a garage; you may own no car! But if the garage contains cleaning fluids in bulk, or the eggs or dusters you sell off your garden stall, someone in County Hall would be interested. As for building on your own property, to create extra rooms, or converting a garage or outhouse, most people would agree with the need for proper plans and inspection and would value the advice of the building inspector or planning officer.

Experience suggests that people in authority tend to be 'no' people; it's the nature of the beast. There are areas where discretion can be exercised, but the tendency may be to justify one's calling and flex official muscle. Tread carefully and watch your back. Small-scale business may not count as change of use – especially if your trade has a low nuisance quotient. Trouble begins when neighbours complain, and once they report you to the council, there is a legal obligation for officers to investigate the complaint. If you plan to run saxophone classes from your mid-terrace townhouse, or smoke herrings in the garden shed watch out!

Permission may be granted or withheld according to the nature and extent of the business, the environmental impact (in the widest possible sense; environmental health officers nowadays monitor noise pollution), whether people are employed, and so on. There is a right of appeal. Proceed without approval and there may be a fine to pay and your business can be closed down or even jail . . . Unauthorised buildings can be pulled down, at your expense, even if they would have passed muster with the planning experts at planning stage!

17

Even this is not the end of the story. Once planning permission is granted, the rating authorities will be notified, and you can find yourself paying swingeing business rates for the part of your home used commercially – you should of course have checked, at the outset, with your mortgage lender or landlord, or by going through the deeds with a solicitor or the Citizens' Advice Bureau, that the business activities you plan are allowable on the property in question ...

What, if anything, can be done, by way of 'damage limitation'? You can certainly involve the neighbours and generally get their approval up front for your mooted business. But tempers and goodwill are fickle things, and friendly neighbours can move out. You could phone council planning departments and have a 'what if ...' conversation. 'If I wanted to do ... [such and such]' what would the official view be?

I know one chap, a designer whose studio, a very stylish but unauthorised development of a tumbledown outbuilding, was being assessed for commercial rates. By chance his musician daughter also used the studio as a practice room and there were guitars and amplifiers around. The designer was able to claim that part of the studio was for domestic use and business rates were levied only on a modest amount of floorspace. Food for thought!

INSURANCE

Insurance needs to be sorted from two aspects: how running your business affects your existing policies, and what new insurance you may need to take out. Once you start running a home-based business your contents and bricks and mortar insurers must be told. This point isn't open to debate. Suppose you needed to claim for some domestic mishap, such as storm damage, or an accidentally smashed antique vase. If the insurer discovered you were running a business from the premises and had not reported this fact, almost certainly you would have invalidated your normal home contents cover and would not be paid out. The same prudent courtesy applies also to motor insurance. Business use cover is not automatic; it needs to be requested, and like home insurance above, you may well find a premium increase follows hard on the heels of honesty.

You may also need to consider some or all of the following types of insurance. *Public liability*. This can relate to any business activity which involves you or your immediate family, and covers possible claims for injury to other people or damage to their property. Your music student's parent trips up on a bit of frayed stair carpet and breaks a leg. You could be the butt of a substantial claim. *Product liability*. You may be a craft worker with high standards. But there could still be a nail left standing proud in your footstool that scars a baby's cheek. *Stock (also goods in transit) and equipment insurance*. Most domestic policies only pay out to a maximum of £1000 or so for an individual item stolen or damaged. Your computer or professional camera kit may be worth much more.

DATA PROTECTION ACT

Any homeworker keeping virtually any information on computer about any living person will need to register under the Data Protection Act. A modest fee pays for three years' registration. Individuals are entitled to see any information you hold on them and to have incorrect information altered or maybe even deleted. If they have suffered materially from incorrect information you have used, you can be liable for compensation. There are fines for not registering.

HEALTH PRECAUTIONS

You need to be fully conversant with the various regulations, which are discussed at greater length in the **catering** section.

As ever there is more to worry about than you may think, and quite rightly so, when you consider the potential public health hazards of cowboy practices in the kitchen! Strictly speaking, the rules apply even if you do not intend to serve food on the premises, but merely make jam or bake cakes to sell at WI halls. Arm yourself with guideline literature (such as *Food Law Inspections and Your Business* and *Success With a Small Food Business*) from the Ministry of Agriculture, Fisheries & Food Mailing Section – Food Sense, London SE99 7TT (Tel. 081-694 8862). And also have one of those non-committal 'what if ..' conversations with your local environmental health officer.

BUSINESS
SERVICES

Secretarial Services

1 FILE NOTES

Background and concept

The home typist or freelance secretary is a familiar figure; so established, in fact, that this type of work, with its steady rewards and ready market, could so easily be overlooked.

At the leading edge of hi-tech, with telephone computer links, such as electronic mail and networked computers, a skilled secretary could handle the business of a global company and never leave home. Realistically, and economically, any suburban or country dwelling secretary could use fax to communicate with city dwellers and mail out hard copy or assignments on disk to be printed out at the office.

If you've got a fax machine you might consider offering fax as a service, commercially, to callers, bearing in mind the need to register the part business use of your home with your local planning department. If members of the public use your home, your insurer will also need to be notified.

Another easy 'add-on' service is phone answering. There's something mightily reassuring about hearing a real, live, warm human voice at the end of the line, not the impersonality of a telephone answering machine.

An interior designer client of mine became convinced he was losing business because prospects and customers who phoned him when he was out of the office, took umbrage at leaving a message on his answering machine. You'd be surprised how sensitive people are, how easily embarrassed when required to 'speak in public', albeit down the phone lines, and improvise into the bargain! More to the point, people are impatient. Hard-pressed callers won't leave a message and they won't phone back either. Instead, they turn to another supplier at the drop of a handset.

Shorthand might be useful for a visiting secretary and for when clients call round. Rather more marketable is to offer a cassette tape transcription service. Dictating letters, articles, books and reports is a tremendous boost for anyone who works with words or needs to communicate on paper. My own output can be quintupled with dictation, though there's a risk that the quality may diminish. I have worked with standard cassettes and a hand-held recorder.

Recorders must have pause and on/off facilities that do not 'advance' the voice after every pause or stoppage. Many businesspeople prefer the more compact microcassettes.

In the long term you may need to 'tool up' with transcription units for at least the common size of microcassette and standard cassettes. You can get on/off foot pedals for ordinary leisure cassette players. But the only way to work professionally, with any pace, is to buy a transcription machine that will take a fast forward/rewind pedal and a stop pedal.

Further associated services for typist/secretaries are proofreading and indexing (detailed work, demanding concentration and an orderly mind, but paying well over the typing rate). See section on **Editing/indexing/proofreading** below. This is all food for thought when it comes to marketing time!

Is this business right for you?

If you can type fast and accurately you may be well on the road to a successful, and interesting, home business.

Interesting? Working for yourself as a secretary/typist is different from working in an office, for a boss: assuming your finances can stand it, you can always turn down tedious tasks!

Even the rustiest skills can be honed to a professional standard or basic skills raised to a respectable level through a refresher course at a specialist college or adult education centre.

2 DOING THE BUSINESS

Strictly speaking, this section doesn't describe lucrative typing but keyboard work. The plain fact is even the most sophisticated electronic typewriter has drawbacks for all but the most straightforward correspondence.

By far the best option is a wordprocessor with a screen big enough for you to see the layout of the page or a page layout preview facility. A hard disk drive and floppy disk facilities are also vital.

You'll want a letter quality printer; some dot matrix machines aren't good enough for smart business correspondence, though they may be fine for rough work, spreadsheets and so on. You should also consider a printer that will handle envelopes comfortably.

Everything you can do to improve your service will count towards reorders and word of mouth recommendations (the best form of advertising). Always ask clients' preferences in margin size, paper weight, and colour, heading and numbering.

Suggest improvements to clients and they will prize your service still more. Here's one tip, for business letters, that's worth a fortune in time saved and temper spared. Type in the addressee's phone number under his or her address. Quite often a business writer sends a letter, then follows it up with a phone call. Having the phone number to hand on your own copy letter saves time looking through an address book or searching back through past correspondence.

Studies show that addressing adhesive labels (on roll or

sheet) and sticking them on the envelopes later is some 25 per cent faster than typing envelopes individually.

How much should you charge? As with any business, you are in a marketplace. Find out what others charge. Pretend to be a client and phone other freelance typist/secretaries. Be prepared to negotiate a reduced rate for bulk work such as an author's manuscript. But don't drop your fees too low for apparently simple work such as addressing envelopes. You may need a cash sweetener to compensate for being terminally bored! Tabulated work and work full of corrections will take you longer and must be priced accordingly.

Get your clients to pay postal charges and phone calls, and be sure paper and stationery costs are either covered in your fees or billed as a separate item. Some typists charge by the hour, but if you're a fast (and honest) typist, that can favour the client, who gets more work packed into the paid-for time. Wordprocessing agencies usually prefer to charge a flat rate according to the type of work. That way time isn't a consideration, and the quicker you work, the more you earn.

Costing by assignment, and fees that include at least basic paper and envelope expenses, are likely to be more enticing in cost-conscious times, because people like to know in advance how much work is likely to cost them. Whenever tradespeople or designers tell me they work by the hour, however low the hourly rate, I feel myself about to sign a blank cheque and back away from employing them (or try to negotiate a deal for the assignment).

Always deliver what you promise. Meet deadlines even if it means staying up until the early hours or hiring someone else to complete a project you cannot handle. Then promise yourself not to overreach in future!

Could you find extra work through an agency? Possibly. But it will feel more like working back in an office again, and you will probably have to pay tax and national insurance out of your earnings. Your most satisfying working relationships will come about when you have personal contact with clients.

If you do register with an agency, be prepared to work at the drop of a hat and at all hours. Agencies have little patience with anyone who says 'no' to an offer of work more than a couple of times; they'll drop you, and never mind the good excuses you had.

3 HOW TO MARKET YOUR SERVICE

Place a window card advertisement in every shop window in your area and near by. Be brave: pay up front for at least three months. The more cash you're prepared to advance, the better the deal you should be able to do with the shopkeeper . . .

Your postcard ad could read:

FAST TYPING SERVICE OFFERED

I type business correspondence, reports, articles.
First-class, reliable personal service.
Collection/delivery possible. Fast turnaround
guaranteed.

Competitive rates.

Phone ....

Type up the card beautifully to reflect the quality of work your customers can expect.

A similar message printed on a leaflet can be sent to bosses of local businesspeople, like doctors, solicitors and publishers. Students and academic staff are big buyers of freelance typing skills for their theses, reports and essays. If you live near a college, ask the secretary to put your small ad or leaflet on notice boards in hallways, as well as in student and staff common rooms. Or place an ad in the college paper.

Academic work, such as typing Ph.D. theses, is slow and painstaking. It has to be clean, perfect and attractively laid out, as your typing will form the 'artwork' that copies will be printed from.

Distribute business cards to friends and relatives to hand around on your behalf. Keep the message simple:

```
           FIRST-CLASS TYPING

           SECRETARIAL SERVICE
```

Your degrees and exam passes are not important ingredients for a business card. What matters are the benefits the prospect can relate to. For example, FAST typing, COLLECTION AND DELIVERY service, FREE EXTRA COPIES.

More ambitiously, place an ad in the classified columns of magazines such as London's *Time Out*, *Private Eye* or *The Author*, the newsletter of the Society of Authors (you will need to get two referees to vouch for your integrity and quality of work).

There are three other writers' journals worth advertising in: *Writers' News*, *Writers' Monthly* and *Freelance Market News*.

HELPFUL READING

Barron's Business English, Andrea B. Geffner, Barron's Education Series Inc (USA), 1982.

Essential Secretarial Studies, Sheila T. Stanwell and Josephine Shaw, Edward Arnold, 1974.

Executive's Business Letter Book, Enterprise Publishing Inc (USA), 1985.

Freelance Market News, Cumberland House, Lassadel Street, Salford, Manchester M6 6GG.

Plain English Course, Martin Cutts and Chrissie Maher, Plain English Campaign, 1989.

To the Letter, A Handbook of Model Letters for the Busy Executive, Dianna Booher, Lexington Books (USA), 1988.

Writers' Monthly, 29 Turnpike Lane, London N8 0BR.

Writers' News, PO Box 4, Nairn IV12 4HU.

USEFUL ADDRESSES

The Society of Authors, 84 Drayton Gardens, London SW10 9SB (Tel. 071-373 6642).

Copywriter

1 FILE NOTES

Background and concept

Before being a designer or a graphic designer became the stylish thing to be, there was the perfectly respectable, if mundane-sounding calling, known as 'commercial artist'. The copywriter is the wordsmith equivalent of the commercial artist.

A copywriter aims to win a response from readers. This could mean writing copy for a poster, to get people to see a play, selling saucepans, 'off the page', via a coupon advertisement, drafting a letter to the press, on behalf of some captain of industry, or preparing the words for a brochure or leaflet and overseeing its design.

My own letterhead lists the following services:

- Brochures
- Leaflets
- Mailshots
- Advertising
- Press Releases
- Design Direction

Is this business right for you?

Copywriting is a lonely profession. Even if you work in an advertising agency, after a briefing meeting with clients, largely managed by account executives, the copywriter is very much left to his or her own devices. A committee can edit copy, but it cannot write copy. If you can master the techniques, learn how to handle clients by yourself and can promote yourself effectively, copywriting is one of the most rewarding – creatively and financially speaking – businesses to run, independently, from home.

Essential skills include typing and the ability to express yourself effectively on paper. Good grammar is a boon, but these days, with spellcheck programs built into computers, great spelling is less of a stipulation. You'll need a word-processor, preferably a computer with hard and floppy disk facilities; the usual phone answering and fax machines are also all but essential.

There are advertising courses; the beauty of copywriting, however, is that you really can learn the ropes through books. My guru Lou de Swart's greatest contribution to my development as a copywriter was knocking out of me the notion that there was something alien or crass about American books on writing. On the contrary, American authors on copywriting are very scientific in their research and generous with their advice, happy to 'give it all away', for the very good reason that, as advertising research reveals, 'the more you tell, the more you sell'.

2 DOING THE BUSINESS

The key skill of the copywriter is arguably the ability to write advertisements. The best commercial writing starts at the top. The headline can make or break your advertisement. Fail to attract the attention of the kind of people you want to read your advertisement and the rest of your work is wasted. The 'body' copy can be a poem of sales technique, but if it isn't read, it's dead.

Your headline should aim to do two things: define your market and promise one or more benefits. Look how simple this can be. A seller of a patent hair growth compound or 'hair weave' system, or a maker of wigs, wishes to attract the attention of potential customers. It only takes one word ...

BALD?

... and a question mark. The benefit – more hair growth or the appearance of it – is implied. That type of blunt appeal is more the domain of the small ads. But the principle is true whatever the scale of the ad. Here's a famous headline from a successful display ad:

How I Retired on a Guaranteed Income for Life

It focuses on its target audience, people who want to retire, and promises a hot benefit: guaranteed income for life. Not bad for less than ten words!

Words matter mightily, but much more important is the ability to lock on to what makes people tick. 'What's in it for me?' is the silent question posed by every reader of commercial copy. Answer that question effectively, and you have an audience and possibly also paying customers.

'Sell the sizzle, not the steak' is great advice to the copywriter. Sell benefits, not product, is another way of putting it. But first you must alert readers that some useful personal information is coming their way.

For this reason the word 'you' is one of the most powerful words you can use in copy. When Yale University surveyed the world's most persuasive words, *you* was followed by *money, save, new, results, easy, health, safety, love, discovery, proven, guarantee*.

There are many more intriguing and important words you can weave into your own powerful ads. David Ogilvy's (advertising supremo) list of words that 'work wonders' includes: how to, suddenly, now, announcing, introducing, it's here, just arrived, important development, amazing, offer, wanted, challenge, advice to, the truth about, compare, hurry, last chance.

Here are other words with proven sales appeal:

absolutely	huge	reliable
approved	immediately	remarkable
attractive	improved	revealing
authentic	informative	revolutionary
bargain	instructive	scarce
beautiful	interesting	secrets
better	intriguing	security
big	largest	selected
colourful	latest	sensational
complete	lavishly	simplified
confidential	liberal	sizeable
crammed	lifetime	special
delivered	limited	startling
direct	lowest	strange
discount	magic	strong
easily	mammoth	sturdy
endorsed	miracle	successful
enormous	noted	superior
excellent	odd	surprise
exciting	outstanding	terrific
exclusive	personalised	tested
expert	popular	tremendous
famous	powerful	unconditional
fascinating	practical	unique
fortune	professional	unlimited
full	profitable	unparalleled
genuine	profusely	unsurpassed
gift	proven	unusual
gigantic	quality	useful
greatest	quickly	valuable
guaranteed	rare	wealth
helpful	reduced	weird
highest	refundable	wonderful

When in doubt over which expressions to use, the copywriter has a simple rule of thumb: 'Write it for the Smiths, and the Smythes will understand it, too'. Simple words can also be powerful ones: God, love, death, free, slim. Also be brief.

Better to use three short words than one long one. Short sentences and short paragraphs are easier to read and understand.

I've talked about the importance of headlines; how do you maintain the interest of the reader ... what next? Easy. You've promised a benefit in the headline, so continue to promise benefits – the more the merrier. Sell benefits, not your product. Benefits are what your product can do for your prospects: happy retirement; peace of mind; money for their children's education and so on.

Here's a tip every pro copywriter bears in mind: tell your prospects exactly what you want them to do. Don't just stick a coupon at the end of your ad, tell them to fill it in. Tell them twice, three times, ten times if necessary. This applies to benefits, too. If something's worth saying once, it's worth saying over again – 'repetition is reputation', is an advertising industry slogan to take to heart.

Copywriters need inspiration, but most of the time they cannot afford to wait for it. Instead, they learn how to 'woo' the muse. That's why reading in bed, studying material last thing at night can be so useful. The subconscious takes over while your active daytime brain clocks off.

You may wake up in the night with a thought or idea or inspiration, so keep a notepad and pen by your side (and in your pocket during the day). You say you'll remember, but time and again you'll discover that it just doesn't happen. That mental 'manna from heaven' just slips away, leaving you frustrated, angry – and poorer.

3 How to Market Your Service

As a copywriter, your ability to market yourself is more than just essential for survival. It's part and parcel of what you do, proof positive that you can probably do for clients what you do for yourself; namely, successfully promote. There are various ways to get your own sales story across.

You can send out letters to decision makers, managing or marketing directors, or proprietors of non-limited companies, outlining your services. Your letter must grasp that 'What's in it for me?' nettle as you start your pitch. You might also enclose some simple, intriguing sales leaflet that also underlines your 'I know how to grab attention' message.

Try this ploy. Send the boss/managing director a critique of his or her current advertising. Don't write to advertising or marketing directors; they're the ones who originated or approved the misguided work in the first place.

Doesn't this upset prospects? Sure, often. But intelligent, constructive criticism is rarely lost on businesslike people. Sometimes you will get a vehement cold shoulder. Other times you will hit home. When chasing your sales letters with a follow-up phone call, as you must, try to win even a brief audience, 'Just give me two minutes of your valuable time'. Then sell the value of your skills and services when you visit.

The thing to watch for with copywriting is the client who keeps moving the goalposts or who seems unsure about his or her requirements. Be sure your understanding and payment relates to an agreed amount of work and that the timing of the assignment is clearly set down in writing.

Occasionally, even after a number of attempts, your copy simply won't gel with a client. But that has nothing to do with being paid. You should expect to get paid for well-directed effort, not for satisfying the client – who may have mistaken ideas about copy or sales angles – and certainly not for the success of any advertising you write. Never get involved in payment that is geared to the response level of the ads you write or the revenue your work pulls in. Monitoring returns and response is far too elusive a task for an outsider.

Another recommended pay ploy, in these straitened times, is to ask for half your fee up front. There is something mightily reassuring about starting with some of the money in your pocket. I always feel that half the money pays for the hard work that is copywriting, the second half is a consultancy fee for my years of experience. If I have to fall down on an assignment, at least my graft should be financed!

The other plus point, of course, is that a client who puts hand in pocket before you start writing shows real commitment, to you and the job in hand. It is also an important step along the road to fast payment at *every* stage.

HELPFUL READING

Better Brochures, Catalogs and Mailing Pieces, Jane Maas, St Martin's Press (USA), 1981.

Confessions of an Advertising Man, David Ogilvy, Longman, 1963.

How to Start and Operate a Mail Order Business, Julian L. Simon, McGraw-Hill, 1965.

My First Sixty Years in Advertising, Maxwell Sackheim, Prentice-Hall (USA), 1970.

Ogilvy on Advertising, David Ogilvy, Pan Books, 1983.

The Craft of Copywriting, Alastair Crompton, Business Books, 1979.

Writing to Win, Mel Lewis, McGraw-Hill, 1987.

Editing/Indexing/ Proofreading

1 FILE NOTES

Background and concept

It's tempting to think of editing, proofreading and indexing as pleasant, relaxing, ruminative work, ideally suited to the free-lance lifestyle. In fact the pace is usually rather hotter, especially within the book industry.

Publishers have trouble enough extracting manuscripts and revisions from authors, and the editing and proofreading stages tend to be last-minute rush jobs, all the more pres-surised given the need to be spot on with accuracy. Indexing is work you can train to do at home, while editing is something you have preferably done or grown into on account of a previous job in journalism or publishing.

Away from book publishing, there is editing work to be had from magazines, especially for the women's market, 'tasting' short stories – deciding whether authors' speculative submis-sions are right for the publication, cutting them back to a specified length (or suggesting ways to expand certain sec-tions), adjusting themes, plot and character types, even down to altering the names of protagonists.

Long articles are also sometimes farmed out to home-workers for editing and proofreading, but you will need to live within striking distance of the metropolis, where most national publications are established. Attractive as the work may seem, it rarely falls to those who do not already have a background or contacts within the industry.

Is this business right for you?

All three skills demand a high level of general intelligence and education. You need to be a great speller, have an eye for detail, and be organised and painstaking; these are slow, careful jobs, even though they often need doing in a hurry!

A bookish or literary background – English degree, author, reporter, book reviewer, librarian, teacher – will help; as will a mind that understands and enjoys working with systems. Possibly a crossword fan might adapt well to indexing.

Indexing is traditionally a blue pencil and card job, but it takes no genius to see how easily it can slot into a relatively simple computer database program.

If you plan on working in the book publishing business, one of the biggest users of freelance editors, proofreaders and indexers, expect to have to travel to London to pick up and discuss assignments with your bosses who, by and large, work in the capital.

2 DOING THE BUSINESS

Editing and proofreading are real hands-on jobs: you need to have been trained under a skilled editor, chief sub-editor or down table sub-editor; this isn't a job that lends itself to book learning, though you can learn proofreaders' symbols easily enough by studying a text and practising with manuscripts or printer's proofs.

As well as checking for literal mistakes (letters of a word transposed), the editor or, more likely, sub-editor, is looking for grammatical and stylistic and typographical errors, as well as checking for potentially libellous statements, copyright infringements and so on.

At a headier level, editing may involve layout or page design, giving titles/headlines to written work, creating cross heads – small headings that break up the columns of text – writing introductory copy, captions to photographs and illustrations, and so on.

Indexing is more amenable to academic study, even distance learning. The Society of Indexers (see below) runs a respected correspondence course. Students need to successfully complete a five-part course before becoming an accredited indexer. The indexing 'graduate' can then submit an indexing assignment to demonstrate the ability to meet the Society's high standards. Following successful inspection of the work, Society registration follows, Registered Indexer being the title awarded.

The Society publishes a journal, *The Indexer*, a regular newsletter and occasional papers, and maintains a library of specialist books at the Library Association's Library. The Society aims to raise standards of indexing and offers a wide variety of services to its members. Its annual publication, *Indexers Available*, lists approved indexers looking for commissions.

Indexing is one of those JIT . . . Just In Time, in business parlance . . . occupations that never the less has to be spot on and comprehensively done. Nothing is as infuriating (certainly to this writer/researcher) than a book that ought to have an index and hasn't, or boasts one that has been cobbled together through lack of time or money. Historically, publishers have saved money by insisting, in their contracts, that authors commission and pay for indexing. Under pressure to behave more equitably, publishers may now be more amenable to sharing the cost 50/50.

Traditionally, the indexer worked with a proof of the complete manuscript, a stack of cards in several colours, and a coloured pencil or highlighter, underlining key words, subjects, concepts, names (not forgetting those contained in the introduction or preface). Diagrams and illustrations are sometimes listed in a separate index, though the Society prefers these to be included in one comprehensive index, differentiated by italics or an alternative font.

Now the process is generally handled in hi-tech fashion, using a computer and a dedicated indexing software program, Macrex and Cindex being among the most highly regarded.

Editors and proofreaders are paid by the assignment or per thousand words, while indexers are rewarded by the hour or by the page but have no further financial interest in the work and should not expect any additional fee by way of royalty or following reprinting.

3 HOW TO MARKET YOUR SERVICE

Editors/proofreaders/indexers can advertise in *The Times Literary Supplement* and *The Times Educational Supplement* and *The Bookseller* magazine. Indexers are advised to consider placing an ad in *The Author*, the closed circulation journal of the Society of Authors. Also write to publishers who specialise in non-fiction books with an academic bias. Outline your experience and any special interest or expertise.

HELPFUL READING

Writers' and Artists' Yearbook (annual), A. & C. Black.

USEFUL ADDRESSES

Society of Indexers, 38 Rochester Road, London NW1 9JJ (Tel. 071-916 7809).

Society of Authors, 84 Drayton Gardens, London SW10 9SB (Tel. 071-373 6642).

Library Association, 7 Ridgmount Street, London WC1E 7AE (Tel. 071-636 7543).

Society of Freelance Editors and Proofreaders, 38 Rochester Road, London NW1 9JJ (Tel. 071-813 3113).

Feature Writer, Syndication Specialist

1 FILE NOTES

Background and concept

This section deals with non-fiction writing, the latter being far more manageable, commercially speaking, than fiction. A freelance news or feature writer can proposition editors – over the phone – with ideas or story outlines. Some of the best assignments and speediest commissions come out of a phone call to an editor. (Remember to confirm the order, quickly, in a letter, if you want to stay in business: editors sometimes change their minds in midstream.) An established writer angling for a non-fiction book contract may be required to produce nothing more than a synopsis, chapter headings and a few sample chapters to secure the deal.

Through experience, editors become pretty shrewd judges of writers. They know that, on balance, a seasoned professional non-fiction writer will come up with the goods; while the beginners and the 'maybes' are invited to deliver the item 'on spec'. As you make your bones as a writer, so the need to write anything speculatively decreases.

The fiction writer, on the other hand, with the exception of the Ludlums and Le Carrés of this world, usually need to write the whole book, story or play before anyone will take their offering seriously.

Fiction writing is essentially a fugitive activity. Even the brightest plot and the most intriguing character can 'die' on the page and be beyond rescue, in spite of rewrites. You never know how fiction is going to turn out until you've written the word ENDS at the close of your piece. Therein lies the fascination with fiction, of course. Imagination – quintessence of being human? – in total, unpredictable control!

The problem is that there are numerous boring, predictable things in life that also have to be handled. Things like bills. Non-fiction is a more quantifiable, businesslike activity, and in a pressurised urban-focused world it's still possible to lead a refreshingly unstructured life, in a pleasing rural or semi-rural location, and make a respectable living as a journeyman/woman non-fiction writer.

Is this business right for you?

Writing is a time-consuming, lonely, head-down activity that takes study, practice and a mean streak: you have to be jealous of what others have achieved and determined to get there, too.

If your brain doesn't spin with ideas, don't bother to pursue writing as a business. Ideas, even good ones, are ten a penny to the pro. Writing talent counts, naturally, but more important is stamina; the determination to succeed; a willingness to work to discover if you have that commercial ability to 'write for a market' and produce what editors like to publish, which may not be what you prefer to write.

My Fleet Street experience shows, time and again, that reliable contributing writers, who can write to a style and a deadline, win out over erratic virtuosos. Anyone can 'break into print'; not many stay the course or earn worthwhile money on a consistent basis.

2 DOING THE BUSINESS

One way to test your ability is to enrol on a writers' evening class or a residential course, such as those run at Missenden Abbey in Buckinghamshire. Or look in *Time to Learn* for details of 'short break' writing courses local to you. (I'll give a free appraisal to anyone who cares to send me work samples and a s.a.e.: Waveney House, 71 Staithe Road, Bungay, Suffolk NR35 1EU, Tel. 0986 894829.)

What are the keys to writerly self-improvement, I ask my students? Silence. Panic. I suggest they answer the question for an activity with which they're rather less involved:

'How do brain surgeons get good at their jobs?'

'Practice,' yells the class swot.

'How? On you?' Point taken.

There are three steps to getting good at almost anything, certainly non-fiction writing.

1. **Study** collect quality writing (articles, 'how to' material), read actively, take notes, write comments in the margins.
2. **Practise** play with words, ideas, writing formats.
3. **Put into practice** send out ideas, see what response you get, what editors say about your work.

Though this may come as something of a shock to the British reader, many of the best books on writing are American. American authors on writing and marketing technique have taken to heart a truism borrowed from advertising folklore: 'The more you tell, the more you sell', and have turned giving away secrets into an art form.

The best technical manual is *The Way to Write* (republished some 20 years later, virtually unaltered, as *A New*

Guide to Better Writing; in itself a kind of object lesson in the power of headlines and persuasive marketing!).

Other writers to look out for are Stewart Harral, Maren Elwood, Larston D. Farrar and Hayes B. Jacobs. Main branch libraries will get hold of virtually any book, even from abroad, eventually. Better still, register your wants with book tracing and out-of-print specialists.

Authors such as these will show you how to brainstorm for viable ideas, how to shape them into marketable commodities, and develop reliable techniques for winning commissions, monitoring output and getting paid.

Only amateurs write articles speculatively; serious writers send out 'soft sell' propositioning letters to editors and then follow through with a phone call or agreed visit.

Writing for profit demands thorough research. Discover exactly what the market wants and how much it pays. Phone publications to ascertain that editors are in fact in buying mode and not fully stocked; ask what types of stories or books they need most.

Type a letter to the editor by name on your professional-looking letterhead. Aim for no more than one side of A4 paper, though you can enclose relevant cuttings, to show intriguing aspects of your story, or photographs. Remember the golden rule in business: be brief; the longer your letters, the longer people will take to reply to you!

Give the letter a title or headline. Headlines are meat and drink to editors. If you can grab attention with a headline they'll be inclined to believe you can 'deliver the goods' in the article, too. On the opposite page is a typical breezy query letter sent to a new BT-backed magazine for business telephone users.

Pictures can clinch a commission. Editors are always looking for complete packages to save them time, money and trouble. Beware you aren't taken for a ride, though; always make some extra charge for your picture-taking skills, even if it's no more than a few pounds tacked on your writing fee, to cover the cost of film and processing.

You don't need to be a skilled photographer these days;

Dear ...

WHAT'S SEE-THROUGH, RED AND BLOOMING?

The old red telephone kiosk I see on my regular trips to Norwich. It stands in a front garden and is used as a mini greenhouse.

I've seen these glazed boxes do duty as shower cubicles . . . drinks cabinets . . . deep freezers . . . bookcases, and more.

Might you be interested in a lively article on this growing market?

I'd include where to buy old red boxes . . . how much it costs to restore and adapt them. A fun piece, in a word, that follows BT's own 'phones are friends' advertising theme.

I use a Nikon outfit and could let you have 35 mm slides or black and white shots, all at a favourable price.

Please accept a call from me in a few days.

Yours sincerely

MEL LEWIS

modern autofocus cameras do most of your thinking for you. A camera that lets you use flash with daylight, to 'fill in' dark patches in a scene or a face, are best; evenly lit photographs make much better reproductions in a newspaper or magazine.

The most common fault with part-time photographers is that they stand too far away from the subject. Step into the picture, so to speak, and fill the frame with your subject.

Duck down to a child's level, rather than shoot from your own standing height.

Instead of taking portraits of people 'flat on', get them to stand sideways, their torso at right angles to yours and then ask them to turn their head towards you. Take shots of BOTH profiles.

Who can you write for? Try the media guides – *Benns*, *Willings*, etc. Publishing books is a slow business and some publication names/addresses will be out of date by the time you read them. By far the best and most up-to-date reference is the *UK Media Directory*, updated via computer database on a daily basis and published six times a year, though you can buy individual copies.

Alternatively, step into any newsagents with notepad and pencil. You don't need to buy magazines or newspapers. Research them on the spot. Cover lines reveal what the editor considers 'hot' news or articles for that publication.

Turn to the contents page. Run down the 'departments' – cookery, consumer advice, personal finance and so on. Department editors may be worth writing to, though regular specialist writers usually supply their copy. More important to you are the titles of special features. Here's where you can make inroads (and money) as a contributor.

Boost your earnings like this.

■ Invest in a wordprocessor so you can rewrite articles quickly, revise thoroughly and sell them to alternative markets.

■ Don't be afraid to send the same idea to a number of editors at the same time. What if they all want your article? Write to me. I'll enter you in *The Guinness Book of Records*. If, as rarely happens (twice in my 28-year writing career), two want your story, provide each editor with same theme stories but approached from completely different angles.

■ Get used to bargaining. Since you rarely know the most an editor will pay, ask what their top professional page or word rate is. An official 'page rate' is eminently burstable for a really hot story, a great picture package or a writer they've taken a shine to. So always try to hike the offered price up, gently, until you meet resistance.

■ Become an expert at something, anything. This gives editors a reason to call you first. Specialists always earn more, as any doctor will tell you.

From a financial point of view, article and book writing is now more badly paid than it was. You can earn a reasonable week's wages for a 1,000-word article from some quarters, certainly the national daily papers, but it's a slog to clinch a commission and most jobbing journalists will settle for £50 per thousand words and upwards for reliable commissions, editors who know their own mind and don't change it too often, and clockwork payment.

Getting paid on time is a bugbear of every business, though writing may be one of the worst. Editors are rarely businesslike; they have 'higher' things on their minds and in fact only rarely are they also cheque-signers.

Money is an embarrassing topic to most people, most of the time, so it's best to be up front about it, clear all aspects of payment and then you won't need to return to the topic (you hope!) later.

Agree a fee, then write and confirm your acceptance of it, together with all the details of the assignment – length of copy, number of photographs (if any), special angles, expenses – when the story is due to be published. The one item of information that you can leave off, to your own advantage, is the deadline.

Shouldn't you ask the editor to confirm the commission in writing ... or wait for his or her letter? Not if you want to complete the assignment before your great grandchildren are christened ...

Your letter is a contract, but it must never read like legalese: imagine the editor was in the room and you were going over agreed points. Talk about 'agreement' or 'understanding' – 'we have agreed that ...'; never use the word 'contract'.

Interestingly, when you get paid is not a matter for the publication. It's up to you. When an editor commissions work, your terms are the ones that matter, unless some other arrangement has been mooted and agreed. It makes sense to mention payment, to clear the air early on. Some editors reserve the right to pay on publication, which can mean never or very much later. Only beginners, trying to accumulate some experience and credentials, should agree to such a stipulation.

Nothing says you cannot ask for part-payment in advance, and where expenses are likely to be high, and borne by you before the publication reimburses you, this is sound business sense.

3 HOW TO MARKET YOUR SERVICE

Take my advice and never refer to yourself as a 'freelance writer'. It has about as much cachet as a 'resting actor'. Writers need to watch their words and their status!

I prefer to be known as a professional writer, or a business or specialist writer – on business, antiques, motoring, how to write and so on. The best titles are the ones publications award you, such as correspondent or columnist, which gives clout as well as suggest tenure; these are the ones to aspire to. When in doubt, simply be a 'writer'.

The point of this preamble? Your most important marketing 'tool' is your letterhead. You'll use your letterhead to send out numerous query letters. My writing guru, steeped in mail order techniques and impressed by the marketing expertise of American non-fiction and commercial writers, suggested my letterheads should have two ingredients: a list of 'credentials', publications I've written for; any writing posts held etc.; and a photograph.

You don't have any credentials, or at least not enough, not the right sort? You'd be surprised how easy they are to 'massage'. One writer, sold on the idea of putting her portrait on paper, said she hadn't written for enough papers. It turned out she had researched for *Cosmopolitan*. That, I insisted, made her a 'contributor to . . .'; she had contributed research.

Another writer was clued-up in a number of departments: finance, DIY and so on, but had never written on these topics. I suggested he bill himself on his letterhead, as a 'specialist in . . .'.

A photograph – a portrait, but it doesn't have to be – cuts a lot of corners for a writer. I tried numerous posed portraits, and then concluded that a relaxed, friendly shot might carry a more sympathetic message. In a scrapbook I found a sharply focused holiday snap taken with my son. The caption read: 'Mel Lewis & Son'. I've continued in this lighthearted vein with one showing me leaping over a traffic bollard – 'Always at the cutting edge of something – Prop. M. Lewis in c. 1962'.

A pictorial letterhead is the nearest your letter can get to a handshake. And for a while having my mug on the masthead also had rarity value. Now numbers of people do it. Television presenter Aminatta Forna took my advice and had some done; MP Diane Abbott uses 'face paper', as I called my personalised letterhead, to distinguish it from plainer paper promoting my clients' products and services.

Another bonus with face paper, of course, is that it cuts a lot of cackle when you phone up to chase a response to your query letter. The editor's secretary invariably knows nothing about your idea, cannot even recall the letter arriving, but when you mention that your paper carried a portrait, she (it's rarely he) immediately snaps to attention.

Not only is the letter recalled, but, often, also which pile it's now in and what the editor said about your suggestion! Hmmm . . . 'How your face can give you a high profile' might very well make an intriguing saleable article!

The second most important piece of marketing equipment is a simple grid system used to monitor the comings and goings of article/book ideas. The grid shows the name of the article, to whom it was sent, job title, name and address and phone number of publication, when sent, when chased and the result. Typically, for an article idea I target five prime magazines or newspapers and send identical letters to the appropriate editors, all at once.

After a few days, but no longer than ten days, I chase the letter with a phone call, and note the comments and response. If I fail to win a commission with those five top prospects I prefer to mail out again with a different idea, rather than try to drum up interest in the earlier, failed idea with a second league of publications.

Marketing through syndication

Writing is a bespoke activity; it's tailored to a market, cut, stitched and tucked according to the style and whims of an editor. At best, your article exactly 'fits' the readership of the publication for which it was written.

This hand-made activity – writing is one of the few hand-made items available in a mass-produced world – ought to be highly prized and handsomely paid. But most of the time it isn't. Syndication, selling the *same* article, news item or photograph again and again, is the marketing scheme intended to redress this monetary anomaly.

Pop record writers capitalise on multiple sales of their songs; authors do, too: the more their books sell, the more they usually make. Syndication enables the freelance writer also to benefit from multiple sales. Whether you have an article worthy of syndication depends on two things: the nature of the article and the rights you have retained.

Copyright is a big subject, but here's a crash course. Your freelance writing is automatically copyrighted to you; it's your 'intellectual property', in legal parlance. You may dispose of – sell or assign – your rights as you wish.

Editors may ask you to relinquish all rights for your writing fee, but you don't have to agree. If the work is good, and the relationship with the editor solid, you should fight for your rights: they could be worth pounds in your pocket.

If you sell only FBSR – first British serial rights – first time

out, you can sell your work overseas, through a syndication
bureau or (not advised for overseas markets) do it yourself. If
you sell an article to a publication with a restricted circulation area, such as the *Yorkshire Post* or the *Hendon Times*,
and only part with area rights, you can market your piece
elsewhere in the UK.

Syndication is big business in America and very little
exploited in the UK. I run a syndication agency and my own
book, *How to Write Articles for Profit and PR*, has a useful
17-page report on the best ways to get into syndication, as a
contributing writer, or as a bureau operator.

HELPFUL READING

How to Make $18,000 a Year Freelance Writing, Larston D.
Farrar, Hawthorn Books (USA), 1957.
How to Write Articles for Profit and PR, Mel Lewis, Kogan
Page, 1989.

How to Write 'How To' Books and Articles, Raymond Hull,
Poplar Press (USA), 1981.

1000 Markets for Freelance Writers, Robert Palmer, Piatkus
Books, 1993.

The Feature Writer's Handbook, Stewart Harral, University
of Oklahoma Press (USA), 1958.

The Way to Write (republished as *A New Guide to Better
Writing*), Rudolf Flesch and A. H. Lass, McGraw-Hill
(USA), 1947.

Time to Learn, A Directory of Summer Learning Holidays,
NIACE, 1993.

UK Media Directory, Two-Ten Communications Ltd,
Communications House, 210 Old Street, London EC1V
9UN (Tel. 071-490 8111).

Writing to Win, Mel Lewis, McGraw-Hill, 1987.

Cuttings/ Picture Library

1 FILE NOTES

Background and concept

A cuttings library can be operated as a low-tech business, with box files and wallets stuffed with well-indexed clippings from periodicals, reports and the like.

Or it can be run using computer technology. The cuttings, scanned into a computer memory, can be quickly recalled to the screen. It's a much faster form of microfiche and far more user-friendly. The cuttings can be printed out in moments or consulted on screen.

Writers, researchers, journalists, politicians and film makers all have a need for this type of information.

Access to a good cuttings library lies at the heart of quick, fact-rich writing for a journalist. I used to spend hours in the old Grays Inn Road *Times* library, by common consent the best cuttings library in Fleet Street. When writing specific commissioned articles for the *Daily Mail*'s Money Mail or Femail pages, I could use Associated Newspapers' library. But without a job on The Street, or accreditation, getting into a good cuttings library is nigh-on impossible.

Picture libraries typically serve book, newspaper and magazine publishers. Here's a typical example. A magazine is running an article on the fiftieth anniversary of the D-Day landings and wants to use that familiar, clichéd, but none the less stirring image of Churchill holding a sten gun, as feisty as any Tommy.

The picture editor refers to library lists and contact phone numbers. Who handles this type of picture? A call clinches the deal.

If there's a rush on, the picture is delivered possibly in less than an hour between London addresses, by motorcycle dispatch rider. If the journal is based out of town the requested pictures will arrive by fast, secure post the next day.

There are general and specialist picture libraries. For obvious reasons it makes a lot of practical sense to specialise. This applies both to cuttings and to a picture library.

Is this business right for you?

To compile a worthwhile cuttings library, you must have an enquiring mind and be an avid reader, with a fascination for collecting and organising information. A librarian or indexing training (see section on **Editing/indexing/proofreading** above) is an ideal qualification. But anyone can get started and learn the ropes along the way.

Setting up a stock picture library is best suited to a photographer (see **Photographer** section below), not least because using someone else's images costs money. If you take your own pictures you generally own all the rights and can dispose of them – in other words, 'lease' them – to clients, as you wish.

In both cases you'll need plenty of filing space and a reasonably welcoming environment, as some clients will want to visit and browse.

2 DOING THE BUSINESS

Cuttings will need to be carefully dated and referenced with the source, as you do them. Use a steel rule and scalpel to remove items from glossy magazines; simply tearing along a steel rule is best for newspaper 'clippings'.

Newsprint fades fast in daylight. You may find a more durable method is to photocopy certain cuttings (always keeping the original). You normally won't part with original cuttings, but merely make them available for study.

If photocopies are also for personal use, there should be no copyright fee or restrictions. If you *sell* photocopies to clients, the water becomes muddier and you will need to talk to a lawyer (try the Society of Authors, listed below) about your obligations.

Running a picture library is better charted territory, but as with most businesses it has its own grey areas, jargon and wrinkles. The *Writers' and Artists' Yearbook*, addressing photographers considering contributing to an outside agency, recommends, '. . . time spent on the presentation of your work, editing for composition, content, sharpness and, in the case of transparencies, colour saturation. . '.

Another recommendation is for succinct captioning of photographs. My own view is that the recommended six or so words is too short by a long haul.

A stock photograph is often one a photographer has taken on their own initiative. But it could equally have been the result of a commissioned assignment or 'shoot' for an advertising agency or magazine, where the understanding is that the residual rights revert to the photographer, once the rights requirements of the original contract have been satisfied.

For example, there may be a stipulation that a picture used in an article is not published anywhere in the same country for six months after it has appeared.

You need to draw up clear and comprehensive terms of business, covering rights offered, search fee, loss or damage compensation, holding fee, reproduction fees, return of work, payment terms, when responsibility for safe handling starts for the client and so on.

The fee is usually linked to the rights sold. Pictures aren't normally sold at all. What is sold is the right to use the picture. Thus, exclusive world publication rights in perpetuity will command the highest fee (and you could still own the picture to show at exhibitions) and the normal one-time rights command a lower fee.

First rights, another familiar request, is the right to publish once only, but before anyone else. Your contract (or, better, 'agreement') should spell out that purchase of rights for publication in one journal does not allow the publisher to feature the picture in another paper in the same group, except on payment of a separate fee.

Rights can also be restricted geographically: first British serial rights is the familiar term in magazine and newspaper publishing.

Quite often a picture editor will ask for more rights than may seem to be warranted. Once you know the ropes (the reference books listed below will help), you will be able to walk that fine line, giving away as little as necessary while not jeopardising sales.

Transparencies are frequently lost or damaged and will need to be properly compensated for. When one Sunday national newspaper lost a famous photographer's consignment of pictures, there was a £16,000 bill to pay.

3 How to Market Your Service

A cuttings library will need to direct its advertising at writers, journalists, researchers and editors. Test response from a classified advertisement inserted in *The Author, Campaign, UK Press Gazette, Writers' Monthly, Writers News, Freelance Market News*. Offer a free leaflet outlining the scope of your library, fees and opening times.

A photo library can mailshot publishers of picture books,

encyclopaedias, newspapers, magazines, greetings cards, text-books and calendars. Other targets will depend on your specialism. If you specialise in photographs of military vehicles you might contact curators of military museums as well as the more predictable magazines with a defence or combat bias.

An amazing amount of material sells simply through listing; but a lot can be more easily marketed where there are good clear reproductions, however small, of the offered photographs.

The time-tested 'winners' that form the backbone of a general photo library remain: children, babies, animals, scenic views and good-looking women. More recent earners are exotic locations, natural history, scientific phenomena and industrial scenes.

Tailor your mailing package along the professional lines of the established picture libraries. A little subterfuge may be necessary to convince the libraries that you are a bona fide potential user of their services. One ploy might be to say you have been commissioned to write an illustrated book on a chosen subject.

HELPFUL READING

Cash from Your Camera, Louis Peek, Fountain Press, 1970.

How and Where to Sell Your Photographs for Dollars, Henry Greenwood (USA), 1960.

How to Sell Your Pictures at a Profit: The Photographer's Marketplace, E. Bennett and R. Maschke, PTN Publishing Corp (USA), 1971.

Professional Photographer's Survival Guide, Charles E. Rotkin, Amphoto (USA), 1982.

The Freelance Photographer's Handbook, Fredrik D. Bodin, Curtin & London Inc. (USA), 1981.

Where and How to Sell Your Pictures, Arvel W. Ahlers and Paul V. Webb, Amphoto (USA), 1952.

Writers' and Artists' Yearbook, A.&C. Black (annual).

USEFUL ADDRESSES

The Author, Society of Authors, 84 Drayton Gardens, London SW10 9SB.

Campaign, 22 Lancaster Gate, London W2 3LY (Tel. 071-413 4588).

Freelance Market News, Cumberland House, Lissadel Street, Salford, Manchester M6 6GG (Tel. 061-745 8850).

UK Press Gazette, Maclean Hunter House, Chalk Lane, Cockfosters Road, Barnet, Herts EN4 0BU (Tel. 081-441 6644).

Writers' Monthly, 29 Turnpike Lane, London N8 0EP (Tel. 081-342 8879).

Translator

1 FILE NOTES

Background and concept

Now that the European Community's much-vaunted Single Market has turned from a dream into reality, there is a renewed call for translators comfortable with at least one of the key European languages – French, German and Italian. Anyone wishing to export or import, or who uses equipment made overseas, could have a need for a translator.

Although the most attractive (and demanding) work might seem to be literary – translating novels, plays, poetry – it is also the hardest to get. The call is much more for translators with a knowledge of technical, medical, engineering, computers, music or scientific subjects, and the pay is on a par with a good trade rate, such as a garage mechanic (numbing but true!).

Those with a command of an exotic language, such as Arabic, Hebrew, Chinese, Japanese or one of the rarer European languages, such as Swedish or Finnish, can expect earnings up to 70 per cent higher.

Since you work for yourself, there is no boss raking off a top-heavy cut – unless you work for a translation agency, when there will be a fee or commission to deduct.

Is this business right for you?

You need to be totally at home with at least one foreign language and have an excellent ability with English. Being able to order food from, or even argue with, a foreign waiter is not what's called for here, but a complete command of idioms, a wide vocabulary, a real feel for word associations and appreciation of shades of meaning, all of which does not come out of any textbook (though you will need plenty of quality dictionaries or even a language degree or translation qualification, the latter being an essential entrée with certain agencies). Faultless grammar is one thing; even more desirable is a sense of style.

Translating ought to be thoughtful, ruminative work, but in reality it is often a 'wanted yesterday' activity. With tight deadlines you'll need to be self-disciplined, reliable and quick, as well as accurate and sympathetic. Good keyboard skills and computer literacy are also highly desirable.

2 DOING THE BUSINESS

Although the most sensible translation route is from a foreign language into your mother tongue, you may be asked to translate either way. Although the mother tongue stipulation seems logical enough, it is not a foolproof benchmark of quality. In the last analysis, a translation into English has to sound like real English, even if it means making certain approximations of mood and sense.

Brushing up or perfecting your language skills has never been easier. There are tapes and records and correspondence courses, such as those from Berlitz, Linguaphone, World of Learning or the BBC. As with most things in life, you get what you pay for: the more expensive courses tend to be better value; they also have a higher resale value.

The headquarters of the Institute of Linguists is the professional body for translators, interpreters and language teachers. The Institute is an examining body and publishes a bi-annual survey on translation fees..

The Translators' Association, affiliated to the Society of

Authors, publishes a leaflet on copyright with hints for literary translators. There's 'live' advice on legal and general translating queries also on offer to Association members.

3 HOW TO MARKET YOUR SERVICE

The *Writers' and Artists' Yearbook*, updated annually, has sound advice for translators seeking large-scale literary or technical work from book publishers. Breaking into this desirable enclave is a bit of a Catch-22 situation: publishers respond unenthusiastically to applications from translators without a track record. You may have to submit an impressive but unsolicited work sample in order to be taken seriously as a contender.

Although the normal pay plan is per thousand words or hourly, as a book translator you may be offered a royalty on top of a fee, though this may only become payable on reprints or second editions.

Yellow Pages will yield the names of translation agencies. Commercial work is best won by writing direct to directors of firms actively involved in import or export to global areas relevant to your own language expertise. The Civil Service and the BBC use freelance translators, and translating jobs are advertised in the journal of the Institute of Linguists.

HELPFUL READING

Writers' and Artists' Yearbook (annual), A. & C. Black.

USEFUL ADDRESSES

The Institute of Linguists, 24a Highbury Grove, London N5 2EA (Tel. 071-359 7445).

Translator

Translators' Association, Society of Authors, 84 Drayton
Gardens, London SW10 9SB (Tel. 081-373 6642).

Credit Controller

1 FILE NOTES

Background and concept

A good many firms, large and small, have a laid-back attitude to credit control – getting in money they are owed. There are many reasons for this: it's embarrassing to chase people for money; most companies are sales-oriented and actually getting in the money is viewed as 'clerical' work; it's easier to go to the bank and extend the firm's own credit.

This last option is the most dangerous, of course: when the banks decide to call in their loans, overstretched business borrowers go to the wall.

Why people don't pay their bills on time, the other side of the coin, is also intriguing and essential for you to understand. The main reason is that *it pays a debtor not to pay up*.

Money owed, but not paid out, continues to earn interest in the debtor's investment account. Or the debtor can borrow less, so still 'makes' money by saving money on loan interest. Possibly one day paying late will be an offence, but right now it isn't, though determinedly slow payment is actionable in court and you will need to bone up on legal aspects.

Late payment isn't always a wilful act and you must be ready to give people the benefit of the doubt. Non-payment may be an accident, or there may be a query about the goods or an unresolved complaint about quality, delivery time etc.

The heart of the service you offer is chasing overdue bills, mainly by means of letters, carefully designed to trigger the pay-up response, and also by telephoning. Your service is a relatively easy sale, since you may choose to offer a commission-only or part-commission system for your own remuneration.

Many firms welcome effective outside help with credit control, finding it hard to recruit willing or suitable controllers in-house. Working with the firm's own headed paper, you become a valued part-time team member. You will need a license to work as a credit controller, details from the Office of Fair Trading, Credit Licensing Branch (Tel: 071-269 8616).

If you are unfazed by the occasional brusque individual, and can 'read between the wires', your score rate will improve dramatically if you spend more time on the phone than writing letters.

Is this business right for you?

Credit collection isn't about being rude, intimidating or even forthright. It's often a matter of being subtle and shrewd, of knowing which buttons to press and keep on pressing.

Slow payers are a nuisance, but not necessarily bad prospects for future business. With the right techniques, you can be instrumental in turning clients around so they smarten up their pay-up routines in the future. And since you may never discover the real reason for slow payment, your letters and conversations must be models of tact and diplomacy, designed to build goodwill, as well as pull in the pounds.

You may need to be hard-nosed, but that's part of persistence, another key attribute of the successful credit collector. Other attributes are good typing/keyboard skills. You don't have to have a computer, but a computer makes you more versatile, efficient and gives your business a longer 'memory'. Basic grammatical knowledge is essential and a way with words is a plus.

When talking on the phone it will need to be against a neutral, businesslike background: no dogs barking, children crying, TV or computer games clattering.

2 DOING THE BUSINESS

The better you understand your 'targets', the more effective
your service will be. A feel for the job is essential, and you
may find yourself becoming something of a psychologist and
detective rolled into one. Just like a medical practitioner, the
'debt doctor' (you) becomes adept at distinguishing the signs
from the symptoms.

Symptoms are the patients' observations about their condition; the signs are what the doctor establishes and records. A
debtor may offer one or more of the following 'reasons' for
non-payment.

1. The cheque is in the post.
2. We've lost your invoice.
3. You failed to quote your order number/our requisition
   number.
4. The goods didn't arrive.
5. The goods were faulty.
6. Your invoice failed to take account of an outstanding
   credit.
7. Your bill includes a discount we took (improperly) on our
   last order.
8. The person who signs cheques is off sick/on holiday/out
   to lunch.
9. One of the cheque signatories is off sick, etc. . .
10. Our computer is 'down'/being uprated.
11. We are being taken over.
12. Annual stocktaking/audit in process.
13. Our accounts are 'with the accountant'.

The real reasons for debtor delinquency are less colourful.

1. The debtor doesn't understand your terms.
2. The boss has great business flair, but cashflow is chronic
   (slow payers are crippling their company, too).
3. Business is great, but the books are in a mess.
4. The boss has discovered that time is money, so is buying
   some with YOUR money!

5. We are too busy with our own business to bother about your business.

In times of recession recovery, every collection letter must have a hidden agenda. Getting past due money in is only part of the picture; retaining goodwill is the other important part. Losing goodwill, and potential future business, is easily done through insensitive handling, impersonal 'voicing' or poorly targeted dunning.

Studies show that a psychological approach has long-range commercial benefits. The easiest part of your business will be sending out 'form' or standard letters, usually graded in intensity, or with a greater threat factor, as time goes on and the money still hasn't come in.

Your skill lies in letters that don't read as if they've been written by robots. You will need to tailor letters to a debtor's profile and circumstances. For instance, a debtor with current payment difficulties, but a history of prompt payments, merits a different letter from a chronically late payer.

Avoid statements that indicate exasperation or a feeling that your own client/boss is being abused. Successful credit collection works on the premise that most people want to pay their debts; that persuasion and perseverance are the best means to get bills paid; and that sarcasm or righteous indignation merely get the debtor's back up.

Here's an example of a letter appealing to a debtor's sense of fair play:

Dear Mr Jones

If I were to ask you what quality you admire and nurture most in your staff you might very well say 'team spirit'. The ability to co-operate, with energy and enthusiasm, is a tremendous plus in business.

When we delivered your drainage equipment a few

---

months ago, we did our part, you'll agree. No doubt you found good use for it, especially in the wake of the recent storms.

Won't you play fair with us, now, and send your cheque for the £2,930 you owe?

Yours sincerely

The following letter probes a different nerve ending. Without actually threatening disclosure of the debtor's name to a credit reference bureau, the hint is there ...

Dear Mr Jones

You have now had several reminders about your overdue account for £465. To date there has been no response.

We are puzzled and not a little anxious about this. From our point of view, naturally, but also from yours. In fairness to yourself you should consider how important an asset your credit standing is.

If you thought about it for a moment or two you would conclude that it is worth a good deal more to you than the amount you owe us.

To protect that priceless asset you need only write or call saying when you will make payment.

Better still, why not send a cheque now?

Yours sincerely

My own book on the topic, *How to Collect Money That is Owed to You,* reveals many more tricks of the letter-writer's trade, such as the importance of the first paragraph and the p.s. in grabbing attention, and the need to use plain language. I never label my invoices INVOICE, instead I call them BILL TO PAY. An invoice is filed and often forgotten, a BILL TO PAY has emotion and 'call to action' built in. Similarly with STATEMENTS, the follow-up reminder to an unpaid bill. Mine are called BILL STILL TO PAY.

There's insight, also, into what copywriters call 'you' copy. In other words, use 'you' and 'yours' all the time, even if it means rejigging a sentence to get those words up front:

Your orders for our goods . . .
You have been paying . . .
Your outstanding balance . . .

They say you can achieve anything with the right form of words. Here's your opportunity to prove and profit from it!

3 HOW TO MARKET YOUR SERVICE

The best way to approach firms for work is to write a letter that both sells your services as a credit collector and highlights their own likely problems with slow-paid bills:

Dear . . .

**NEW CREDIT COLLECTION SERVICE
LOW FEES. HIGH MARKS FOR
GETTING IN OVERDUE CASH!**

Are you spending enough time collecting money owed to your business?

> Probably not. You don't have the time. You're too busy building your business. On the other hand is ANYONE in your firm free to devote enough time to do the job properly . . . as successfully as you would like?
>
> I specialise in writing collection letters that build goodwill as well as pull in cash. I'd be happy to work with you to devise correspondence that is exactly right for your business and your type of slow payer.
>
> I use only proven techniques and charge remarkably low fees . . . etc., etc.

Say you'll call a few days after sending your letter (first-class), and do it. Try to get an interview over the phone and offer to take with you some samples of your work. Never discuss other clients. Confidentiality is vital; besides, this also gets over the hurdle that you may have just started and have no clients as yet!

You'll need a neatly designed, professionally printed letterhead: a laser-printed or DTP-designed letterhead won't do. Consider giving your business a name, but never pretend to be grander than you are or imply that you are a company if you are not a legally constituted limited company.

Consider something along the lines of:

**THE EFFECTIVE CREDIT COLLECTION BUSINESS
HIGH SPEED CREDIT COLLECTIONS**

How much should you charge? As much as the market will bear, consistent with being competitive. Research the competition. Be open about what you are trying to do. Talk to editors or news editors of the credit journals listed below.

Ask to be sent any helpful literature, and ask the journalists if they know of anyone offering a similar service, what they charge and how they operate.

HELPFUL READING

Credit and Collection Letters, National Association of Credit Management (USA).

Credit and Collections for Small Business, David R. Kitzing (USA), 1981.

How to Build Goodwill Through Credit Correspondence, Luther A. Brock, National Association of Credit Management (USA), 1976.

How to Collect Money That is Owed to You, Mel Lewis, McGraw-Hill, 1982. Available, price £3 post paid, direct from the author at Waveney House, 71 Staithe Road, Bungay, Suffolk NR35 1EU (Tel. 0986 894829).

How to Collect the Money you are Owed, Malcolm Bird, Piatkus, 1990.

USEFUL ADDRESSES

Institute of Credit Management, The Water Mill, Station Road, South Luffenham, Oakham, Leics LE15 8NB.

CREDIT JOURNALS

CCA News 0244 312044.

Credit Control 0277 225402.

Credit Management 0780 721888.

Bookkeeper

1 FILE NOTES

Background and concept

A bookkeeper is to an accountant what a classroom assistant is to a teacher. A bookkeeper holds the fort, keeps order and generally manages things – in this case the payroll, petty cash, PAYE, receipts and invoices, and anything that pertains to figures and associated paperwork.

You must be *au fait* with PAYE taxation and VAT regulations, and will need experience/training or qualifications or both to be able to present the accountant with balanced books come tax year end, when the figures need to be prepared – verified and/or given the stamp of approval before being filed with the Inland Revenue inspector.

Your choice is to work in-house for independent professionals or work in- or out-house for businesses, charging an hourly rate plus expenses.

Bookkeeping is an ideal home business. Outlay and equipment costs are minimal, after purchase of a suitable PC; even software accounts packages are reasonably priced these days.

Is this business right for you?

This is meticulous work that demands concentration, a clear mind and a numerate brain. You'll need somewhere private to work, with guaranteed freedom from interruptions.

Patience, reliability, honesty, integrity (references will

certainly be requested), accuracy and clear handwriting are all stout personal recommendations.

Security is essential, too: you'll need a strong, locking cupboard or filing cabinet for confidential documents.

Since your paperwork is irreplaceable, as well as 'sensitive', part of your value to a client will be your personal service, travelling to pick up work and bringing it back by hand. Unless you live in a location with reliable public transport connections, car ownership is a must.

2 DOING THE BUSINESS

General secretarial skills, together with bookkeeping experience, may rate as highly with a prospective employer as specific accountancy training. Good grades in maths and English to at least GCSE level would be a meritworthy basic qualification.

There is a two-year BTEC diploma and a one-year general certificate in bookkeeping, both part-time studies. Or you could investigate one of the several home study (correspondence) courses on offer (information from the International Association of Book-Keepers).

As a bookkeeping 'returner' looking for a refresher course, consider one of the college courses run under the aegis of the International Association of Book-Keepers.

With bookkeeping, expertise and qualifications are far from academic: an unqualified bookkeeper who misrepresents her or himself and lands a company in the soup may be liable for negligent misstatement and be sued by the client; in this respect, you would be wise to look into professional indemnity insurance.

The computer side of your business also needs to be looked at closely. You'll be looking to purchase a PC, printer and suitable software. The first step – especially if you are out of touch with (or have never been *au fait* with) computers, computer jargon and specifications – is to talk to helpful, knowledgeable salespeople with a talent for plain talk.

Also read up on the various packages on offer. Sybiz Windows may be one user-friendly contender and certainly the Sage Sterling packages (Bookkeeper, Financial Controller, Cornix Simple Accounts II) come well recommended.

Many software companies offer training on particular products – a much better bet for a would-be professional than trying to wade through a manual. Training is a great way to learn all the corner cutting tricks in a day or two.

3 HOW TO MARKET YOUR SERVICE

Go for the direct approach where possible. Mail a query letter offering your service to managing and financial directors, or proprietors, by name. *Yellow Pages* are a good place to start your targeting exercise.

Follow up with a phone call, between three and seven days later. Offer to call in and meet, no obligation, no fee. The personal touch is vital every step of the way; besides the honesty of your face will need to be seen to be believed . . .

Try classified and semi-display advertising in the business section of a well-regarded local newspaper. As a member of business self-help groups, Rotary and Lions Clubs, and the like, you'll meet prospects in a social atmosphere.

The next time there is some new fiscal legislation looming, or a change in the VAT rate mooted, offer a free seminar to local businesspeople. It's a great way to retail your services and relay your credentials.

Aim to provide a regular service, possibly a visiting service (for farmers, garage owners, vets?), where you either pick up their financial papers on a regular basis or go in to their premises on a specified day. Continuity is the name of the game, and there are few jobs in which you can quickly become as indispensable as in bookkeeping.

HELPFUL READING

Accounting World, available from The Publishing Dimension Ltd (Tel. 071-872 5522).

USEFUL ADDRESSES

The Association of Accounting Technicians, 154 Clerkenwell Road, London EC1R 5AD (Tel. 071-837 8600).

International Association of Book-Keepers, Burford House, 44 London Road, Sevenoaks, Kent TN13 1AS (Tel. 0732 458080).

Newsletter Editor/ Publisher

1 FILE NOTES

Background and concept

If you ever dreamed of editing, owning and running your own newspaper or magazine, the newsletter is that opportunity writ small. Small, that is, in terms of print, staffing and distribution costs; there may none the less be potential for sizeable profits.

Newsletters cover many businesses and interests: new business opportunities; financial services; interior design; retailing; antiques fairs; haute cuisine restaurants; media and communications; personal presentation skills; air cargo and freight forwarding; labelmaking.

The essence of a newsletter is, well, news, but with a fine and narrow focus. For example, there are plenty of articles on marketing in the weekly trade papers for marketing professionals, but rarely anything that focuses, on a regular basis, on marketing for morticians and aromatherapists or sheet-music sellers.

Identify a viable niche market and you can build a steady income, a nice life and, that great rarity in home employment, a saleable commodity, when the time comes to retire or change course. One British investment newsletter sold for a reputed £1.25 million.

Is this business right for you?

You need to be literate, preferably with computer skills. A background in journalism, publishing, communications, design or marketing would be a boon.

2 DOING THE BUSINESS

Success in newsletters is often about angles. Find the right one, often a surprise slant on a familiar and favoured topic (like money), and the market can open up. A great angle is rarely obvious. Nor is it often 'exciting': some of the most successful newsletters have lacklustre written all over them. Yet something intrigues, tickles the imagination and sets off that blessed reader response, usually voiced thus: 'By golly I *need* that information.'

Howard Penn Hudson, publisher of *The Newsletter on Newsletters*, and author of the book, *Publishing Newsletters*, describes the principal categories of subscription newsletter as follows:

1. Investment letters, of interest to investors and business-people with funds to juggle.
2. Business letters, the busiest aspect of newsletters by far, providing specialised information for a carefully defined audience, typically interested in publishing, economic conditions, environment, chemicals and so on.
3. Consumer newsletters, aimed at a mass market, but still specialised, e.g. the *Harvard Medical School Health Letter*. Cookery, eating out and travel are topics that are also high on the agenda of consumer newsletter publishers.
4. Affinity newsletters, focusing on popular but not universal interests, such as fishing, photography or gardening.
5. Instructional newsletters, which resemble self-help books divided into digestible supplements or a correspondence course in self-improvement.

Here are some successful newsletter titles, mainly from America: *Januz Direct Marketing Letter*; *Kovels on Antiques and Collectibles*; *The Newsletter on Newsletters* (essential reading for an overview of the market, new contenders etc.); *Real Estate Investing Letter*; *Beer Marketer's Insights*; *Smart Money*; *Product Safety Letter*; *Car Rental/Leasing Insider*; *Crime Control Digest*; *Contest Newsletter*; *Tax Angles*; *Growing Child*; *Air/Water Pollution Report*.

Penn Hudson finds that after two years in business some 50 per cent of newsletter launches are still successfully breaking waves. The proprietor of *The Hideaway Report*, focusing on holidays and travel, walked away from a high-level government job to start his paper, and in 1990 decided to peg his circulation to 'just' 15,000 copies at US$85 per copy.

How frequently should your newsletter appear? Probably more often than you think is the short answer. Experts at the American Newsletter Association say high frequency is often the key to top dollar success – at least once a month is advised.

Since newsletters are often run at a loss in their early days, and only start to make money with repeat subscriptions, it's as well to note that weekly newsletters have the best record for renewals; fortnightly publications come next, and monthly newsletters fare worst, though the best monthlies can boast renewal rates of 80 per cent.

Most newsletters are in A4 format, for posting convenience (an A5 envelope comfortably takes a newsletter gently folded once, and creasing and damage, in transit, is minimal) and also because A4 is a convenient shape for desktop publishing (DTP).

Traditionally, newsletters were always word-only documents. Now image-making is a very accessible part of DTP publishing, thanks to Windows drawing programs, Adobe Illustrator software, Apple Macintosh computers and laser printers.

How much should a subscription cost? Price-setting is critical to newsletter success, and as much as the tendency is for would-be publishers to overestimate the tally of subscribers, so it is also common for them to underestimate what the market will bear by way of price.

There is a rule of thumb for working out the optimum price of subscription, once you have studied your 'universe' of potential subscribers and guesstimated the total number of prospects you can hope to reach. Ten per cent of this figure is the number newsletter professionals work with.

Now write down the sum of money, based on promotional costs, expenses, fees and so on, you need to achieve to have a profitable business. This is your gross income. Divide the 10 per cent (or similar) subscriber figure into your gross figure to find the asking price of a subscription. If your subscription price looks too 'top heavy', and your other figure-work is sound, perhaps your initial optimism in the title is unfounded!

Mind you, if your mooted newsletter is targeted to sell to executives, you may be able to charge more. People are always more willing to pay more when someone else – in this case the company – is footing the bill.

3 How to Market Your Service

Half your budget should go on marketing, ideally; no less than 30 per cent, at a pinch, while the publication is in its launch stage. Since profit may not be forthcoming until renewal time, some publishers are prepared to plough back in all putative profit just to get more subscriptions coming in, ready to reap the profit harvest a year or more on.

There are many rules of thumb associated with direct mail, but the one that concerns us most here is the 2 per cent rule. This says that a response of 2 per cent is about the best you can expect on average. Some of the most active direct mailers work with a lot less than this and still make pots of money. But they mail out in huge numbers and enjoy economies of scale that are beyond the reach of most humble

newsletter publishers. Industry research gives a number of
guidelines:

- the majority of newsletters require a universe of 20,000 to
  100,000 targetable prospects to stand a fighting chance of
  success;
- well-financed publishers are happy to spend £1 to get £1
  and will cheerfully forgo profits until renewal time;
- rich publishers pour money into newsletters until they
  reach the crock of gold;
- your first results – in a properly researched and planned
  campaign – will be your best results, for if you don't hack
  it then, you probably never will;
- offer a free sample or free report;
- offer a low price report or sample;
- always send a (preferably personalised) letter with your
  package;
- every mailing must ask for a subscription;
- enclose several pieces of literature in your mailing;
- print on different colour (slightly tinted) paper;
- don't staple or pin documents.

HELPFUL READING

How to Launch a Newsletter, The Newsletter Association
(USA), 1990.

How to Start and Operate a Mail Order Business, Julian L.
Simon, McGraw-Hill, 1965.

How to Write Articles for Profit and PR, Mel Lewis, Kogan
Page, 1989.

How to Publish a Successful Newsletter, CommuniCorp.

Publishing Newsletters, Howard Penn Hudson, Charles
Scribner's (USA), 1982.

The Gutman Letter, Walter Gutman, The Something Else Press (USA), 1969.

UK Media Directory, Two-Ten Communications Ltd, Communications House, 210 Old Street, London EC1V 9UN (Tel. 071-490 8111).

Telephone Sales

1 FILE NOTES

Background and concept

Telesales is the jargon name for this occupation, in which people phone prospects to sell them goods or services.

Telesalespeople don't enjoy a very good reputation. They're the callers who wrench you away from your dinner guests to listen to a tedious script, boringly intoned, in a bid to sell you double glazing you don't need. Or fitted kitchens, or bedrooms, or stone-cladding, or to tell you that your house has been chosen to be a showhouse for some new-look decorative technique that sounds like it's going to be free but somehow never turns out that way.

The approach, and the products, vary, however. Telesales people can be 'order takers', who check availability and prices of goods, using a computer or catalogue, occasionally selling callers on alternative lines when their first-choice items, or colours or sizes aren't available. Or they can be highly trained individuals with a lot of product knowledge and advanced interpersonal skills.

Often the telesales people (frequently women, who are less threatening, more empathetic and better at telephone marketing) aren't trying to sell anything at all, merely attempting to qualify prospects, so the real sellers, the technical experts, can move in later for the hard or long-haul sell.

My motorcycle dealer client uses a telesales expert to detect serious interest in a specific make of motorbike and book test rides. The showroom salespeople then try to close the sale after the ride.

In America, the annual spend on 'professional telephone marketing' topped US$34 billion in recent times. The British are only now waking up to the potential of the technique. Is the telephone really that powerful a sales tool?

Consider this. You go into a store to buy a suit or a dress. The phone rings. Who gets asked to wait ... You or the caller? Nobody. The caller automatically gets priority over the 'live' customer. Nine times out of ten, the store assistant won't even bother to excuse the interruption *or* ask if you mind waiting. Even though *you*, not the caller, are the hot prospect for a sale! Even though you are both in mid-conversation or the salesperson is in mid-spiel!

That's the awesome power of the phone.

Is this business right for you?

You need a good, clear speaking voice. Roedean or Eton accents are not normally required. 'Regional' accents are perfectly acceptable – provided people can understand what you are saying.

You'll also need good hearing, a confident, unflappable manner, a nice line in chat and the kind of persistence that makes people smile and keep listening or responding, rather than grimace.

One expert says this is 'very much a people business ... You need to have a gut feeling about people, to put yourself in their place ... A brain is essential equipment.'

Anyone with a background in reception work, amateur dramatics or courier experience, perhaps, could prosper in this field. Working for a company who would provide training, you might need GCSEs in maths and English.

2 DOING THE BUSINESS

As an independent, or working for a telesales company, you can either operate from home or work from client offices. A professional I consulted, with years of successful experience in financial services telesales, says she prefers to work from client offices: 'I walk around with a cup of coffee and drink in the atmosphere. I don't mind my phone calls being overheard. I like playing to an audience!'

The real problem, she says, is that most people don't have the discipline to keep going when working at home. Then there's the phone bill to consider. It's almost impossible to monitor or cost calls accurately in a way which will convince a client you are scrupulously honest. It's much easier to charge an hourly rate, or a rate per number of calls or contacts, and use somebody else's phone.

Should you work from a script or ad lib? The expert says she never reads from a script. You could try working from bullet point notes. Each bullet/asterisk/number/letter has a one- or two-word message that acts as a memory jogger. It's the same technique people often use when speaking in public.

Rejection makes teleselling psychologically hard work. You must learn how to keep going when others will have been 'negged' into inactivity. The classic case of the 'negged' seller is in the life insurance business. Persistence is the name of the game. There are numbers of techniques to help.

Try standing up to make your calls. One life insurance company, which shall be nameless, used to encourage its cold-calling salesforce to stand on the desks to gain an even greater psychological advantage! The floor does fine, however, and standing does help you breathe better. Their other recommended procedure was to refer to a manager for some instant training or reassurance.

3 HOW TO MARKET YOUR SERVICE

For obvious reasons, the best way to sell this service is doing what comes naturally: intriguing clients over the phone. Once you are started and successful, the business tends to snowball through personal recommendations.

Businesspeople who have completed a particular telesales assignment for their own company have no qualms about passing the name of a good self-employed worker to a friend in need of similar services. The thinking seems to be that keeping that person busy, out of PAYE employment, and in circulation, means they will be around for future assignments.

HELPFUL READING

How to Increase Your Sales by Telephone, Earl Prevette, Chartsearch, 1958.

How to Win More Business by Phone, Bernard Katz, Business Books, 1983.

Successful Telephone Selling in the '80s, Martin D. Shafiroff and Robert L. Shook, Harper & Row (USA), 1982.

Telephone Selling Techniques that Really Work, Bill Good, Piatkus Books, 1990.

CHILDCARE AND EDUCATION

Exam Coach

1 FILE NOTES

Background and concept

An exam coach enjoys the best of both worlds. Helping students to pass national school exams, nevertheless, you do not have to put up with the widely acknowledged flaws of the State system – over-large classes, rowdiness, unmotivated pupils, mountainous paperwork, and so on.

Stories abound of parents living frugal lives, selling their cars, trading down their homes and going without holidays in order to pay for their children to go to private schools. Very many more parents are happy to pay to have their children coached through GCSEs and A levels. Private school pupils and adults are also potential candidates for private exam coaching.

Is this business right for you?

By and large this business is only suitable if you have a formal teaching qualification. This could be a teaching diploma, degree and add-on teacher training year or a B.Ed. degree.

Although there is no official monitoring of exam coaches and private tutors (and why not?), parents are well advised to insist on qualifications such as those mentioned and also to ask to see original certificates as evidence of attainment.

There *are* cowboys around and no private coach worth

their salt should object to providing the type of proof that would (or should) be requested in any job application.

2 DOING THE BUSINESS

Many of your pupils can be coached in your own home, which is very much more cost-effective for you and probably less distracting for the child. As it may not be practical for the child's parent or guardian to go elsewhere for the duration of the tutorial session, you would need a warm, comfortable drawing room to accommodate them.

The essence of this type of work is one-to-one teaching, so that even teaching twins the same subject would be a diverting and potentially counter-productive division of labour. Where a parent insists or where it is feasible – with some music or foreign languages, for example – you could consider a raised, rather than a double fee for multiple tuition.

Depending on your catchment area your age range is likely to centre on children aged 9 to 13 years old. You will need to be totally *au fait* with the curricula in your special subjects and also with general changes in school teaching.

There is currently a strong call for help in the subject of English, partly because of the National Curriculum and also because coursework now contributes towards examination final marks. Also, parents are rightly concerned to see grammatical, legible and properly-punctuated work throughout the year.

3 HOW TO MARKET YOUR SERVICE

Expect a pre-exam hiatus in your work and market accordingly for this peak period call on your skills. Cards announcing your services should appear wherever parents or students gather – libraries, kindergartens, playgroups, libraries, church halls, sports and leisure centres, swimming pools, student noticeboards etc.

Also, consider booking modest advertising space in your local paper and, if appropriate, given where you live, in *The Times Educational Supplement, The Times* and the *Daily Telegraph.* One coach had remarkable success with an advertorial feature in her local paper.

An advertorial is normally glib puffery, limply disguised as editorial. Traditionally advertorial is cobbled together by reporters who are embarrassed and/or angry about being obliged to write blatantly biased copy. In this case the coach wrote her own story, full of direct quotes and familiar, friendly copy that addressed issues of abiding concern to parents.

She paid rather more than the price of straight advertising space, as is typical for advertorial, but was rewarded with an unusually high response – 'people warmed to the fact that there was something of me in the piece'. Basking in the success of her efforts, she now operates mainly on referrals.

One of the problems with this type of freelance work, of course, is that there is no continuity: having passed their exams, your ex-pupils go off into the wider world and have no further use of your services.

If the referral system proves too slow or too passive for you, you might try asking satisfied parents to put a few words of recommendation down on paper. Nothing boosts confidence so much for a client contemplating using your services as being given a few phone numbers of parents who will testify to your probity and the quality of your coaching.

As schools are discovering to their cost, it's one thing to teach subjects according to guidelines, quite another to be able to show a reassuring track record of exam success.

Another option and source of work is to register with one or more of the educational agencies, such as Gabbitas Educational Consultants.

HELPFUL READING

How to Do Better in Exams, Barclays Bank (leaflet), 1989.

How to Take Examinations in College, J. N. Hook, Barnes & Noble (USA), 1958.

Learn How to Study, Derek Rowntree, Macdonald, 1970.

Passing Examinations, Clifford Allen, Macmillan, 1963.

Teaching Students to Learn, G. Gibbs, Open University Press, 1981.

USEFUL ADDRESSES

Gabbitas Educational Consultants Ltd, Broughton House, 6–8 Sackville Street, London W1X 2BR (Tel. 071-734 0161).

Music Tutor

1 FILE NOTES

Background and concept

It's never been easier to learn to play a musical instrument. If you don't know what modern electronic keyboards are capable of, step into your local music shop in a commercially quiet time and ask for a demonstration.

I popped into my local pub last night, and discovered a keyboard and guitar duo on stage. In days gone by their sound would have been thin indeed. Not today. Since the keyboard had bass lines programmed in for all the tunes in his repertoire for the evening, and could successfully mimic a saxophone, percussion, accordion, church organ, electronic and grand piano, and every kind of string instrument, the guitarist was all but redundant.

Learning to play a keyboard is nothing if not fun. Also – and this is no mean point when it comes to teaching children – you can buy keyboards in sizes that small fingers can cope with; nowadays, nobody ever need be put off by the problems of reach experienced with traditional piano ivories. You can even buy keyboards that have full-size (seven-and-a-half octave) scales and are, thanks to some miracle of technology, touch sensitive. And modern keyboards don't weigh a ton either.

I labour on about keyboards and the piano, because this is by far the most 'orchestral' instrument to play and teach. Musical structure is literally at your fingertips – and the student is obliged to learn both bass and treble clefs. Once any finger stretch problem disappears, and the student can make clean notes, he or she can concentrate on playing music.

Try telling that to the finger-sore guitarist, who at least has frets to mark out the notes, or worse, the violinist who is obliged to create notes from scratch each time.

This heartfelt lament comes from a former professional guitarist and guitar teacher, a.k.a. the author of this book. But of course you should teach whatever instrument you can competently play and for which there is a market.

There is a growing call from schools for itinerant music teachers and a good market in private tuition. I suspect that today there is less emphasis on gaining Grade examinations and more on being musically literate to a hit record standard. So be it. Someone who enjoys reading Jilly Cooper may eventually get round to Joseph Conrad; similarly with Elton John and Elgar.

Is this business right for you?

You'll need to be an accomplished musician, preferably with a visible track record – certificates, diplomas and so on. All help convince adult learners and parents that you know your stuff, but a rousing audition would serve the same purpose.

As a travelling tutor you may need to be mobile, especially if your instrument is cello or double bass. If children visit you, be prepared to have mum or dad or a minder loiter for the entire lesson. In this case a warm, comfortable drawing room is a must, as you don't want them in the same room, cramping your style and that of your pupil.

2 DOING THE BUSINESS

Some years back, when I was teaching guitar and writing about music, I formulated a revolutionary theory of teaching music. Under the inauspicious title 'Guitar Topsyturveydom', the theory (it applies equally to teaching any instrument) was published in a sleepy, anachronistic, but much-loved little paper called *B.M.G.* – Banjo, Mandolin, Guitar.

I quote: 'Guitar teaching is upside down. Let me tell you how. The guitar student pays his teacher cash. He is buying a service. And, as with other paid-for services, the customer would expect to call the tune. But the guitar student – and what I'm saying here concerns especially the adult student – doesn't.

'Far too often he takes what he is given, instead of asking for, and getting what he wants and is paying for ... I wanted to be able to accompany songs; learn a mere half dozen chords I could substitute in any blues sequence ... pick out a few licks to add colour to my folk playing ... Some of my teachers couldn't do what I wanted to do. Nor could they teach it ...

'What I really wanted was often so small, I felt sure it was within my grasp. But my teacher would act as if I was working up to a Wigmore [Hall] debut! ... the guitar teacher should have a similar function to a consultant in business or medicine. He [or she; this was 1971] should be a paid expert who tells you what you need to know.'

Food for thought? Most of your younger pupils will want to go for Grade exams, those of The Associated Board of the Royal Schools of Music being the most prestigious, though awards from Trinity College of Music and the Guildhall College of Music and Drama are also highly rated.

As a private teacher you may be eligible to become a member of the Incorporated Society of Musicians, an élite self-help organisation which sets minimum charges, advises on tuition agreements, and publishes a register of private tutors and other literature designed to encourage a high level of professionalism. It also provides legal support.

The music tutor is at the mercy of the pupil who starts out keen, but whose interest wanes as the work gets harder. To overcome this potential commercial handicap you might consider charging a fee to cover a programmed course – ten lessons, lasting forty minutes to an hour is common – and ask for full or part payment in advance.

I began teaching guitar to one ten year old and was then asked to include his eight-year-old brother in the sessions. When mum balked at being asked double the fee, I cut it back to one-and-a-half times my going rate. For bigger groups you might get away with double or even two-and-a-half times your normal hourly charge; don't be slow in pointing out the bargain this represents for individuals who share the overall fee for the session.

With some noisy instruments it helps to live in a detached property, though even that might not be sufficient protection for neighbours. Upset them and you might find yourself on the receiving end of a visit from the environmental health officer and even the planning department, who would not normally be concerned with your musical activities.

3 HOW TO MARKET YOUR SERVICE

Write direct to the heads of schools and principals of colleges offering your visiting tutorial services. Include suggested programmes for study; name any students of yours who have achieved good exam results or gone on to perform or teach; offer to audition and even run a sample – free? – tutorial or workshop, to get the feel of the place, and tune into students' needs and interests.

One of the most promising marketing angles of recent times is offering to teach music to adults who were told as children that they couldn't sing.

Making headway in a private teaching marketplace is via the familiar route of shop-window cards and placing ads in the classified columns of local newspapers. If stage performance is your forte, consider putting on a show, possibly for parents of a particular school or schools, and if necessary at your own expense, in order to hand out self-publicity material announcing that your musical services are available to their children – for a price.

HELPFUL READING

Guidelines for Independent Music Teachers, Maggie Teggin, published privately.

'Private Teaching as a Career', Incorporated Society of Musicians Information Sheet 03/5 (see below).

USEFUL ADDRESSES

Incorporated Society of Musicians, 10 Stratford Place, London W1N 9AE (Tel. 071-629 4413).

Childminder

1 FILE NOTES

Background and concept

Looking after someone else's children, on a day-to-day basis, seems to have a lot going for it. Especially for a housebound mum with her own pre-school children to care for; and sure enough, with more women than ever going back to work, this is a boom period for childminders in certain parts of the country.

As with many businesses, however, there is a lot more to this than meets the eye. Some of the restrictions and council strictures are caring and sensible, while others are pedantic.

Is this business right for you?

You'll need a comfortable, accommodating home, with good catering, toilet and wash facilities. Hygiene, health and safety are prime considerations, and anyone who is overly house-proud should consider another home business.

There may be some equipping to do (curiously, you do not have to be a mother to become a childminder): potties; high chairs; cots; play-pens; small chairs and tables; plastic cups and saucers, knives, forks and spoons; climbing frames; clothes for dressing up; simple musical instruments; TV and video; felt picture kit; 'wet' painting kit; crayons; books; play-dough; jigsaws.

You'll need to attend a number of courses and throw open

your doors for quite searching inspection by the authorities (environmental health officer, health visitor and so on), on a continuing basis.

2 DOING THE BUSINESS

The rules of registration – you must be registered with your Local Authority to mind children – make intriguing reading for a winter's evening:

> A requirement of the registration is that the above named person must not receive on to the premises more than five children under the age of eight years, of whom no more than two children are under five years of age. Of the children under five years of age no more than two may be under two years of age. No more than eight children in total under fourteen years of age may be cared for at any one time. Such children will include the childminder's own or any other children in the household.

A friend decided to become a childminder. She wanted to start quickly but had to wait for a place on one of the induction/training courses held only a couple of times a year. The choice was to attend for a couple of hours for five consecutive evenings, or do a day-long intensive course.

She found that only an hour and a half was devoted to looking after children, and a good deal more devoted to principles and standards, quality of care, tax and National Insurance, insuring yourself and your property, and the registration process. She later went on a first aid course for two hours a week for five or six weeks.

Health checks included inspection of her refrigerator and a study of detritus in the carpet. The social services also check childminders, their family and any lodgers.

She was obliged to install a fire blanket and extinguisher, and fix a lock on a hall landing window considered unsafe, even though a child would have needed to stand on an adult's shoulders to reach it. Otherwise, the precautions and checks relate, sensibly, to heat and light, fire, catering, ratio of adults to children etc.

As a matter of course, you will need to keep records of all your charges: contact phone numbers for parents; names, addresses and phone numbers of the children's doctors; essential medical notes on each child, such as allergies or special diets.

Is all this worth the trouble? My friend was hampered by her wish to mind children only while her own kids were at school and to limit her work to termtime. This has proved impossible. She says childminding is a workable, even a lucrative occupation, if you are prepared to treat it as a business, rather than an affair of the heart brought about by the fact that you adore children.

The Government no longer sets out charges for childminders, but instead publishes a thorough survey of fees reported across the UK. A *Negotiating Guide for Childminders* reveals the highest quoted fees (for the year to January 1994), predictably for Greater London, were £4 per hour, £135 per week. In East Anglia this dropped to £3.20 and £128. The median figure for the two areas were, Greater London, £1.60 and £70 and for East Anglia, £1.50 and £64.

The rules of natural justice say there should be more money on the table for evening, overnight or weekend minding duties; in the real world this is harder to achieve.

Guidelines say you should charge for times when a child is on holiday or sick and doesn't require your services: 'You have reserved a place for your child and ought to pay a retainer.' In practice this takes a steel-hooped heart to accomplish.

To cover those times when you, the childminder, are off sick, the suggestion is that you befriend other childminders who can step into the breach to help (and take your fee) and you help them on a reciprocal basis.

Joining the National Childminding Association offers entitlement to professional insurance.

The NCA has also published a useful booklet, with headings such as, Prepare your own children, Some parents can be difficult, Settling in new children, Children who worry you, Potty problems, Eating problems, Destructiveness and aggression, Neglected and abused children, Tantrums, Emergency and illness, Food – Special diets.

3 HOW TO MARKET YOUR SERVICE

As a registered childminder you are put on a social services list for referral to families looking for minders. But this only works if there is a call via this channel. You are allowed to advertise, in newspapers or via shop window cards. It pays to mention that you are registered and you must make the registration document available for inspection.

USEFUL ADDRESSES

National Childminding Association, 8 Masons Hill, Bromley, Kent BR2 9EY (Tel. 081-464 6164).

Music Group Leader

1 FILE NOTES

Background and concept

Why set up a traditional children's playgroup when a music group offers exclusivity, learning, teamwork, exercise and fun, all at the same time?

In one such scheme, established in a number of church and community halls, children (brought by a parent or minder, who stays with the child) enjoy an hour-long session in which they sing, dance, recite, play musical games and more. The structure of the session, duration and location can all be varied, according to response, your own circumstances and available facilities.

The music group idea arose out of a friend's frustration when she tried to set up a playgroup/baby-minding centre within her large London home and was told that the beautifully renovated basement she'd planned on using was a fire risk – this in spite of it having French windows on to the garden at one end, a door leading out into an areaway with an iron staircase at the other end, plus staircase access to the rest of the house in the centre!

She decided instead of running a playgroup to try a music group. Working with a friend (both women have children of early school age) she ran them in church and meeting halls, within a five-mile radius of her home. The groups were an instant sell-out success, and now provide a useful cash income, independence and a good measure of local celebrity for both women.

Their publicly declared aim is to 'develop the children's musical vocabulary, while adults learn how to stimulate their children musically – something they can put to good use in their own homes with a child "who doesn't know what to do next"!'

Is this business right for you?

Training as a dancer, musician, nursery nurse, nanny, teacher, youth worker or playgroup leader would be a clear advantage. You need to be agile, musically inclined, though not necessarily academically trained – there is no need to be able to read music. The work is physically demanding and, if numbers are high, it makes a lot of sense to work with a colleague who can share the load, and organise and monitor smaller groups.

A cheery, patient disposition is a must: some children don't adapt readily to the jolly, co-operative atmosphere and some adults get fidgety even if their offspring love every minute.

To run such a business from a detached home, you would need a large sparsely furnished room, an outbuilding or garage space, which would need to be carpeted, lit and heated. Expect to invest in the peace of mind insurance gives against the children getting hurt, your own property being damaged (your existing policy probably will not cover property, given your professional activities). Planning permission may also need to be sought.

Alternatively, you could run the group from a hall. This should be warm, dry and preferably detached from surrounding buildings. It will need good, natural light, a comfy carpet or springy wood floor and an electric point.

2 DOING THE BUSINESS

The music group in question is limited to under-fives, but that rule is not carved in stone. These pioneers use an electronic keyboard (a guitar, accordion or traditional piano would do almost as well) and a variety of genuine percussion instruments – maracas, cymbals, tambourines – and improvised ones, some suggested by the children.

The advantage of the keyboard is that it can be programmed ahead of the session; tunes, pauses, even voices, can be prerecorded. Free from anxiety about wrong notes, timing and so on, the leaders are better able to concentrate on involving the children, encouraging response to the music and the rabble-rousing physical aspect, which children adore. You can use traditional or home-made music, pop songs, nursery rhymes, whatever suits.

3 HOW TO MARKET YOUR SERVICE

A snappy name, possibly something with a musical flavour to it, will help. The original group launched itself with a press release to the local and national press, together with portraits of the two founders. The story began as follows:

NEW UNDER-5s GROUP TUNES UP TO
THE MAGIC OF MUSIC

At last! A playgroup designed to bring out the music and rhythm in your child . . .

The organisers created an attractive A4 poster, using a Compaq computer, Windows software and a laser printer, and placed it where mothers might see it – in crèches, post offices, libraries and so on.

Depending on the affluence of your area, you might consider charging say £1 to £2 per session, per child. As the sessions caught on, and the leaders wanted to expand and be confident the numbers would hold up – or at least the revenue would, to pay for the rental of the venues – they decided to ask for payment for the whole of the term in advance. Their sessions operate only in term time because the leaders are themselves mums with children to amuse in the holidays. I envisage a lively market for music groups in vacation time, possibly for a play-leader without children or with older children.

The music group organisers I know have been arranging for the printing of special T-shirts to sell to the children in their groups and help promote their music sessions in the wider world.

Adult Education
Tutor

1 FILE NOTES

Background and concept

Almost every county of Britain has its adult education (AE) centres, usually located in schools, sometimes in a building or complex reserved for adult learning (such as the famous Wensum Lodge on the River Wensum in Norwich, which also boasts a rare residential facility), or even the lounge of a pub.

Classes are held mainly in the evening (from 7 to 9 p.m.) and on selected Saturdays throughout the year in term time, when a centre may open its doors to a dozen or more different 'crash courses' held between 10 a.m and 4 p.m. Daytime learning is a weaker tradition, but is developing rapidly.

On Saturdays, students, or 'learners', in AE jargon, are invited to bring their own lunch, with tea, coffee and snacks usually available. An evening class course of study, one night a week, normally, can extend from 6 to 10 or 12 weeks and even continue through the year, provided there is sufficient student interest in maintaining the class.

Alternatively, a tutor may structure a short course, and run it more than once in the term or start anew in subsequent terms with fresh sets of students. High demand subjects – such as foreign languages for beginners – often merit quick repeat treatment.

Sadly, going to 'evening classes', an endearingly British tradition, has recently taken a body blow, and is a victim of cutbacks. Officialdom favours practical learning, 'vocational' classes leading to exam qualifications. Funding has been cut and centres are now obliged to think commercially and to market themselves in an uncharacteristically hard-headed fashion. In a word, they have to be self-sufficient.

Course fees have gone up and attendance figures slumped accordingly. However, there are 'concessionary' reductions for those who are out of work, full-time students (not over 19 years old), disabled people, those on income support and so on.

The money paid to tutors is quite respectable. However, a tutor trainer invited to read this chapter, prior to publication, pointed out that in certain subjects where there is a large element of planning or homework, in terms of hours actually worked the rate may drop much lower.

Travel expenses may also be paid. I live in Suffolk, but being in a 'border town' work also for Norfolk centres. Norfolk Council ignores the first 20 miles of travel to work per teaching session; in a rural area that's par for the course, they reckon; thereafter they pay a rate per mile.

Is this business right for you?

Tutoring is an ideal part-time occupation that can easily produce a reasonable income if you are prepared to travel and play the field to secure a string of classes.

Teaching is much harder work than is generally appreciated. If you relax on the job, the class clocks off mentally and physically. An unenthused adult class reacts badly; they don't come back!

And you may not get invited back either . . . I managed two two-hour teaching sessions in a day through one term, but with a 60-mile round trip to get to one class, it was very hard work. If your energy levels are low, especially when you might normally be relaxing after dinner in front of the telly, give this one a miss.

You don't necessarily need a degree or to have had any kind of teacher training or even teaching experience to apply to tutor at an AE centre, though all of these things may help convince the centre heads that you are capable of carrying the part. Exceptions to this rule of thumb are when the tutor applies to teach languages or GCSEs; centre heads may prefer graduates.

What is required is knowledge of a marketable subject (or subjects; I teach antiques and non-fiction/business writing), a desire to pass it on and a tutorial manner that adults will respond to.

2 DOING THE BUSINESS

You'll need to plan your course and submit a copy of this low-key syllabus to the centre head for approval. Handing the syllabus out to members of your class is also an exercise in keeping your own teaching promises!

Adults learn – choose to learn, by and large, since no one makes them attend evening classes – for a variety of reasons, not all of them obvious. Adults learn differently from young students; AE teaching has its own skills and disciplines.

Of course there's likely to be a 'lust to learn', but other surprising and subtle motivations may also play a part in bringing adults into the classroom. One council's induction pack for new tutors points this up vividly, with quotes from students along these lines:

'I joined an evening class because I felt lonely . . . and needed the social contact.'

'I felt myself becoming nothing more than my husband's wife instead of a person in my own right.'

'When my husband died, I realised what a sheltered life we had been leading. I now pride myself on being an expert in eighteenth-century miniatures, a fluent speaker of bad German and an interested spectator of the Arts.'

Students and tutors alike suffer 'first night' anxieties. Tutors are given advice on 'ice-breaking' techniques, which also help people (tutors included) learn everyone's first name.

A tutor who taught counselling said one of his favourite routines was to ask volunteers (you rarely 'go round the class' in kindergarten fashion; adults resent being put on the spot) to explain how they got their names.

An A-level maths tutor offered the teddy bear tactic. Students start off with name tags on their chests. The tutor produces a teddy, or some other soft toy, throws it to a class member, then shouts out a name. The toy holder has to pass the teddy on, the faster the better. The name stickers are removed and the game hots up.

The aim is to relax people, to have a laugh, with none of the po-faced head-down competitive compulsion of the stereotype classroom. Adults can be as shy as children, but are far less able to release that tension and anxiety. An adult who feels the strain may simply fail to attend the next class.

Instead of asking individuals in turn to introduce them-selves, what they do, what level of knowledge they may have and why they're attending the class, split the class into 'part-nerships'. The partner probes gently for all this information, then does the honours on behalf of his or her interviewee.

Getting class members to relate to each other, as well as the tutor, is a priority also when teaching starts. The induction literature spells it out: 'Sometimes use small groups. The smaller the group the greater the opportunity for each person to talk.'

When teaching hallmarking on antique silver I invite the class to bring in their own silver trinkets, plates, ornaments etc. (always bringing in some of my own as a failsafe). I do my explanation bit on the board, then split the class into groups of three or four, and issue each group with a magnifying glass, hallmark chart and unfamiliar silver items.

Novice AE tutors must attend induction courses and there are opportunities for (free) formal training leading to recognised industry qualifications. Right now I'm taking a 40-hour City & Guilds 7306 Part I course. There's a longer Part II course and the further option of working towards an AE teaching diploma.

3 HOW TO MARKET YOUR SERVICE

Your library will point you in the direction of your local AE headquarters; ask there for a list of AE centres, names of centre heads, and their phone numbers and addresses.

The best time of year to apply for work is March, but there may be opportunities any time in the term. Write a letter of introduction or phone and make an appointment. Before agreeing to see you, the head may send a form asking what subjects you might teach, at what levels, any academic qualifications, relevant practical experience, when you are available and so on.

If you don't get that reply, keep phoning. Names, like flowers, wither unless kept fresh, according to one perceptive writer on this topic.

You can apply to any number of centres, but beware of 'double-booking' the evenings you wish to teach and which may be available. Friday nights are generally a washout with AE evening courses, though day classes may run successfully on Fridays.

What are you going to teach? A local 'Carry on Learning' leaflet reveals the following courses on offer:

Double-entry bookkeeping	Bobbin lacemaking and needlecraft	Computers for beginners
Water and reflections	An introduction to heraldry	Tracing your ancestors

Cake decorating	Advanced cake	Folk guitar for
Looking good	decorating	beginners
from top to toe	Assertiveness	Clock repairs
Everything you	training	
want to know about		
gardening organically		

Saturday workshops include:

Classic car restoration	Hairdressing	Wordprocessing
Flowers in the home	Beginners' chip	workshop
Batik/space dyeing/	carving	
natural dyes/block		
printing		

In among the evening courses are GCSE and A-level classes in German, Spanish, social studies, maths, business studies and English, as well as RSA accounting and bookkeeping courses.

In addition to a reduction in attendance figures, the refocusing of adult education, under its new pragmatic directive, may also have knocked out some of the more whimsical topics traditionally on offer – the ikebana, macramé, candle-making type of class.

At a recent enrolment night my antiques class, due to start in a few days, was bursting at the seams, but my writing course numbers were predictably low.

Most courses won't run unless there are a dozen or so students in the class. The antiques subscription looked to be a humdinger and, in the event, the writing class, with its seven students, was allowed to run in a kind of trade-off that centre heads are sometimes able to make if they can still balance the books.

Discuss your choice of teaching topics with the centre head. Modern favourites include computer studies, wordprocessing and classes associated with exam courses. The next stage is vital, and can make all the difference between success and failure to run a class.

Who publicises wins is the simple message for prospective

AE tutors. Months before teaching starts centre heads are busy preparing publicity 'pick up' material to hand out to libraries and other civic centres.

There may also be a major splash of publicity closer to enrolment time. The message goes out from centre heads to tutor hopefuls: can I have some background material on you; a few selling words about your course (space is often strictly limited; a 15-word curfew is not uncommon); any illustration material ...?

Deliver the goods fast and you may win pole position on the publicity page. If you have your own ideas for handing out publicity, special 'ins' with commercial organisations, the possibility of 'piggy-backing' a mailing going out to members of a local club, for example, go for it. Bear in mind that privately originated publicity needs to be vetted for quality, accuracy, taste and so on, by the centre head; it may need to carry your local area logo and the name of your centre head or area supremo.

I was trying to set up a course in motorcycle maintenance for a biking friend. Take-up was slow and time running out. With help from the college, I produced a publicity leaflet and handed it out at a nearby race-track. I attended classic and custom bike shows, and stuffed hundreds of leaflets into the handlebars of motorbikes. The result? Almost more people than we could handle!

HELPFUL READING

Adults Learning, Jenny Rogers, Open University Press, 1971.

Adult and Continuing Education, Theory and Practice, Peter Jarvis, Croom Helm, 1983.

COMPUTER
SERVICES

Desktop Publishing

1 FILE NOTES

Background and concept

Desktop publishing (DTP), an intriguingly modern way to make money from home, using computer equipment, has been given an unfair press – not least in the section on **Computer Design,** below.

The point is that the ability to shape a clean-looking page of text, more or less on autopilot, using a computer with a wordprocessor facility and a DTP software program, and to label the cover of the resulting document with a couple of expanded and contrasting typefaces on the laser or bubble-jet printer, does not a designer make.

The two skills should not be confused. A DTP specialist, like a jobbing printer offering a good, low price, efficient publishing service, is worthy of hire for those reasons alone. That said, the more tasteful or eye-catching a DTP operator's work becomes, the more his or her fame will spread and the money flow in.

This chapter deals with the two main aspects of DTP. First, there is the inputting and publishing service you may offer to others, using your computer equipment and basic layout skills. Typically, brochures, text-heavy advertisements, reports, wordprocessing, CVs, booklets and posters are the mainstay of the desktop publisher.

Next there is the very different notion of DTP, which involves designing, printing, publishing, marketing and distributing information for profit. It may also involve writing original material for self-publication.

This type of DTP is the modern equivalent of the eighteenth-century pamphleteer, though with a rather sharper commercial edge and greater self-sufficiency: thanks to technology, we can write, print and publish, leaving home only to go to the post-box for distribution.

Publishing simple, but usually highly focused, information for a popular market is quite rightly regarded as one of the quickest routes to financial independence. Provided your information is 'right', in the sense that it really does strike a chord with the knowledge-hungry populace, and that all the other aspects of your business – costs, pricing, advertising – are also on target, there is worthwhile money to be made.

One of the often-cited examples of self-publishing success stories is that of Joe Karbo, the man who put his name to the book, *The Lazy Man's Way to Riches*. I say 'put his name to', because Karbo – shock, horror – allegedly didn't write the book. He paid someone to do it for him.

Is there anything wrong with that? Not in the real world there isn't. Does the shoe shop manager need to make the shoes he or she sells? Should health food shops sell only bread they themselves have baked?

The imploding irony of the *Lazy* book is that it talks about making a fortune doing precisely what Karbo has himself done: selling information via mail order – a fine example of making pots of money by giving the rulebook away with the game!

Is this business right for you?

The qualifications for journeyman DTP work are similar to those needed for computer typesetting (see p. 126), without the need to understand the arcane symbols and commands that operate typesetting equipment.

The point about DTP is that the whole job is done by you

on screen. A basic feel for design is easily reinforced by some serious reading of the mind-expanding design books mentioned in the **Computer Design Service** section below.

Contrary to belief, spellcheck programs do not let the poor speller off the hook entirely; the near dyslexic will find the computer as flummoxed as they are, though the word alternatives offered by the well-meaning, but otherwise clueless, computerised thesaurus may brighten an otherwise dull day!

Understanding printer's marks is scarcely essential, since all of your corrections can be made on-screen – often I simply ring mistakes in ink on the printout to save time, since it's obvious enough what's wrong when you arrive at that point on the manuscript.

But the ability to spot mistakes, the proofreader's sharp eye for grammatical errors, literals (key slip-ups), an alertness to potentially defamatory statements and breaches of copyright, are all skills that must be cultivated to survive and win in the DTP business.

Whether or not you have what it takes to make a go of self-publishing is a rather trickier question to answer. Beginners anguish over what they take to be the critical question: 'What shall I publish? What topics sell?' This is the easy part: you simply suss out what the competition, established desktop publishers, offer as regular fare and produce your own variation on a theme. Writing ability is also a non-essential part, as we have seen. What does count, in spades, however, is marketing savvy.

2 DOING THE BUSINESS

Anyone who can type accurately, at a reasonable rate, who owns a reasonably advanced computer able to run a DTP program, and who owns (or has access to) a laser or bubble-jet printer, can set up as a desktop publisher.

As you progress you may want to enhance your repertoire with programs that enable you to choose a wide variety of typefaces at the touch of a button, or draw on-screen in a freehand fashion, using a special program and a mouse. A colour monitor and colour printer will let you preview the colour work your jobbing printer will produce. And a scanner can turn images – photographs, drawings and even transparencies – into computer-usable information that can be incorporated into your reports, leaflets and books.

Most of the information you need to equip your home office and progress will come out of studying computer literature. *Desktop Publishing by Design* (albeit angled towards Aldus PageMaker software) is a good jargon-buster for DTP terms. The book also explains typefaces, point sizes and graphic design techniques, as do the many computer magazines on the bookstalls.

However, don't subscribe to these magazines or buy blind. Pay a visit to a big newsagents and run down the computer magazine 'coverlines' for DTP and related topics. Then turn to the articles in question and check there's enough relevant material to justify purchase. Reviews of new DTP software are obviously essential reading.

Bear in mind that bookstall magazines are product oriented: the publishers make their money by attracting advertisements from hardware and software manufacturers and retailers. You should also investigate the more 'academic' publications dedicated to your interest; such as *Desktop Publishing Commentary*, *Desktop Publishing Today*, *DTP User* and *Text and Image News*.

The next step is to visit a computer/software showroom at a quiet time and get a patient, knowledgeable assistant to put the programs through their paces. Remember to ask for programs to be run on computers that are no more powerful than yours. A computer freak friend can help with technical points later in the day, after you have made your purchase or you can use the free hotline often provided as a courtesy service to software purchasers.

Your ability to produce good, clean copy, and an attractive page layout and presentation is just as important as being able to key copy in fast and accurately. Any respectable DTP program will do most of the design thinking for you and let you adapt certain aspects of layout to suit your preferences or the needs of your client.

Publishing your own (or someone else's) material is the other side of the DTP coin. I have written DTP reports anonymously for a publisher (*How to Make Yourself, Your Product or Company Famous*; *How to Write and Test Powerful Display Advertisements*; *How to Launch a Newsletter*; *How to Write for Love and Money* etc.). Your lesson is easy enough to grasp. The secret lies in the 'How to' slant of the titles. Lock on to a deeply felt human need or desire, such as how to be better at business, enjoy rude health, attract the opposite sex and tell people how to answer that need or fulfil that desire.

3 How to Market Your Service

DTP, as an advanced wordprocessing service, is a classic case for small ad self-promotion, possibly with leaflet drops to local businesses and follow-up phone calls.

Your printed material has to be your 'left hook' in quality terms; you'll sell on the neatness and impact of the publicity you produce. Your chasing call has one aim: to arrange a 'no obligation' meeting. Take with you samples of your work, including work you've done for other clients, and the more famous they are (even locally) the better. Don't worry about confidentiality; your new prospect is going to glance at the sample, at best, not read it.

Clients usually have little enough idea about what style of presentation they want or perhaps they know but can't put their wants into words. By taking a goodly selection of samples and formats, you can clinch sales without wasting your valuable time.

Most DTP publications (you are now wearing your DTP publisher hat) are sold via mail order; I've listed a number of excellent books on mail order, below, to help you get to grips with that fascinating study.

Because DTP books/reports/pamphlets tend to go out through the post, publishers may take liberties with the appearance of their publications. From the point of view of customer confidence and repeat sales, this is poor marketing, bad business.

Karbo's book is a genuine square-bound paperback, with a professionally designed cover. But because the book never needed to stand on a bookseller's shelf, the title doesn't appear on the spine. It may be the only book on my shelves with an untitled spine, but it's still very hard to find at a glance!

The best method, from a presentational point of view, is to attach stiff card covers, back and front, possibly with a cut-out 'window' on the front to show the title printed on the title sheet beneath, which saves having the covers expensively printed. My preference is to use comb binding (you can buy a comb binding machine for well under £100), spiral or ring binding (such as that used on shorthand notepads) or a rigid plastic spine to hold the pages together.

Start your DTP publishing empire with one or two good strong titles. Buy classified space in a proven-effective medium for this type of item, such as *Exchange & Mart*. Selling 'off the page' is possible; you may have more joy, though, with enquiry ads which you follow up with a leaflet that sells your publications in bullet-point form, trumpets the credentials of the author, the efficacy of the 'how to' techniques and perhaps includes a glowing testimonial letter from a satisfied reader or practitioner of the techniques in your manual.

As your publishing 'list' grows you will be able to justify the price of display advertising and invite readers to tick the titles they wish to receive and fill in the order form below before enclosing their cheques.

HELPFUL READING

Desktop Publishing Commentary (journal), Pira International, Randalls Road, Leatherhead, Surrey KT22 7RU.

Desktop Publishing Today (journal), (Tel. 0622 858251).

DTP User (journal), (Tel. 0956 229466 or 081-777 2735).

How to Make Money with a Home Computer (Carnell DTP report), John Lawson Neale A.C.I.S., 1991.

The Lazy Man's Way to Riches, Joe Karbo and Richard G. Nixon, FP Publishing (USA), 1973.

USEFUL ADDRESSES

Carnell Ltd (DTP reports publisher), 37 Salisbury House, London Wall, London EC2A 5PJ.

Merlin Publications Limited (DTP reports publisher), Unit 14, Hove Business Centre, Fonthill Road, Hove BN3 6HA.

Chartsearch Limited (desktop publisher), 28 Charles Square, London N1 6HT.

Computer Design Service

1 FILE NOTES

Background and concept

Graphic design is a profession that is in the ascendant, thanks to the new computer design packages and easy-to-follow software. Designers trained in the old school method of using freehand drawing, rub-on Letraset etc. are discovering they can boost their output many times over, working with any of the Apple or DOS-based software design programs, such as QuarkXpress and Adobe Illustrator, using a mouse to draw.

People in business, especially, used to commissioning old-tech (pre-computer era) designers for their leaflets, brochures and reports, will welcome the flexibility, speed and often more reasonable prices of computer-based design.

In a curious way, the proliferation of computers, and basic computer and keyboard skills, has made people more conscious of design, page layout, typefaces and so on, more alert to the look of top-class work, giving the service you plan to offer a fighting chance of success. Those who have paid for a DTP service, and been disappointed with its amateur appearance, are prime prospects for the quality service you intend to offer.

Is this business right for you?

Given the right equipment, it is relatively easy for anyone with half an eye, an ounce of design know-how, and who has spent a couple of hours with the desktop publishing (DTP) software manual, to typeset and design a page to parish magazine standard. But that's not what professional design is all about.

Designers may well be born, not made. It's the instinctive sense of balance, proportion, and feel for the 'right' size and style of typeface that comes with natural visual good taste; all the rest is the honing that comes with training and the dexterity that results from practice.

Art students may make good designers, if they can steel themselves to think commercially, and of course there are graphic design courses to consider.

Unsure of your aptitude? Give yourself a real shot in the arm; read Bob Gill's *Forget all the Rules About Graphic Design*. See if/how this revealing book inspires you.

A creative job with cachet design may be, but in the real world, it is a head-down occupation, with a risk of eyesight problems, repetitive strain injury and all the other ills associated with protracted VDU use.

Designers do get out of the house to see clients, naturally; but for the money-motivated ones who get good at their job, visits become an unfortunate necessity of life, given that instructions for a good number of assignments can be transmitted by fax, without the need for time-consuming personal contact.

The most successful designer I know earns money as long as he's at his desk, twitching his mouse and gazing at the Mac. He resents 'flesh-pressing' exercises and is generally successful in getting client meetings to take place on his home territory. I suggest you do the same.

2 DOING THE BUSINESS

With so many manufacturers trumpeting the features and benefits of their products, and some hardware being rendered obsolete by the company that produced it in less than a year (just six months, in the case of laptop computers, according to a report in *The Times*), it must pay you to do some serious homework before signing any cheques.

You don't need state-of-the-art equipment; you can buy an Apple computer, suitable for basic design for about £700 at this time of writing, and a typesetting contact told me of a top notch design program being sold for £40.

Remember, however, that slow operating computers will limit your output and lead to frustration. Besides which, a low powered model may not be able to take updated software or run certain programs.

Should you choose an IBM-compatible design system or one from Apple? My own feeling (and I run both a DOS-based system *and* an Apple in my publicity office) is that Apple is considerably more user-friendly but more expensive, given that your range of compatible printers is severely limited and subsidiary hardware is pricier, though getting cheaper.

If you do a lot of keying in of copy you might be better off with a non-Apple model: I've yet to come across an Apple keyboard that could match a Compaq (Contura 3/25 laptop) for sheer typing speed or ergonomic comfort. Nevertheless, the two most prolific and talented designers I know both swear by Apple. Try to get both systems on long-term evaluation loan and see how you get on.

My favourite designer, a former printer, started his design career seven years ago with a 512k Amstrad and then invested in an AppleMac SE with Adobe Illustrator software, an Apple laser printer (still his workhorse printer after nearly five trouble-free years) and an Abaton scanner (since superseded by a more advanced model).

A scanner acts like a computerised photocopier and feeds images, such as a photograph or a drawing or logo, which need to be incorporated into the design for an ad or a letter-head, into the brain of the computer.

That package – in its day at the cutting edge of technology – set him back £10k in the mid 1980s. Equipment of comparable power and sophistication costs only half as much today, thanks to astonishing advances within the computer industry.

Four years ago my designer friend upgraded to a full colour Mac II computer (which lets you see how colour work will look when printed) and, in a bid for total independence, added an Agfa Studio Set 200 image setter and an IGP-1 RAS processor to his studio (in reality a tiny extension to his modern semi on a housing estate).

These last two items enable him to complete the last stage of design work without leaving the house. Now he can supply the bromide, which looks like a black and white photograph, or the film, the negative counterpart, from which a printer produces printed work.

He also earns useful money acting as a bureau for other local designers and typesetters: they use his equipment to run out their own jobs to bromide or film. The entire studio package cost some £30,000, so it needs to earn its keep!

On top of acquisition costs, there are servicing and maintenance fees to pay. Unable to find an economical contract to cover his computer, this designer decided instead to buy an economy Apple, a Mac LC, to act as back-up, should his main computer fail.

Not only was this a cheaper option, but now his wife uses the 'spare' computer to input copy while the wizard works his on-screen design magic!

3 HOW TO MARKET YOUR SERVICE

Copy success, said my one-time boss and mentor Trevor Deaves. He's right: it saves time and grief. My designer friend started out with a blank screen and now drives around in a top-of-the-range Volvo. Perhaps his marketing system could work for you, too.

His first step was to produce a king-size business card that listed all the services on offer: typesetting, design, artwork, paste-up, line drawing. Next he mailed 40 people a week, eight per day, and followed them all up with phone calls: 'It seemed like a good number,' he says, 'and it worked. One of the best times was when the new *Yellow Pages* came out. It was full of leads. I still try to keep up with *Yellow Pages* to trade up and find bigger and better paying clients.'

The phone calls had one aim: to locate a print service buyer and fix an appointment: 'I hated every minute of those visits, but I did them anyway!'

Once he'd bought the advanced Apple outfit, the business card was dropped in favour of a newsletter which had more space to show what could be achieved using the design program. He also added corporate identity and illustration to his menu of services.

His charges are based on what has to be paid out each month. The separations needed for colour printing will cost extra, since they cannot (yet) be produced in-house.

His success comes from quick turnover, 'wanted yesterday' work. The range of clients is vast: from a nuclear power station to a chain of hotels, a motorcycle dealer to an egg box company!

As well as artwork for printing on to card or paper, he provides designs for silkscreen printers and transfer images for a ceramic pottery company. He sees a growth area in specification sheets for estate agents, and site plans for builders and developers, assuming a strengthening economy!

HELPFUL READING

Advertising and Agency Skills, Tom Cardamone, Watson-Guptill Publications (USA), 1981.

Editing for Print, Geoffrey Rogers, Macdonald, 1986.

Forget All the Rules About Graphic Design, Bob Gill, Watson-Guptill Publications (USA), 1981.

Preparing Art and Camera Copy for Printing, Henry C. Latimer, McGraw-Hill (USA), 1977.

The Design Concept, Allen Hurlburt, Watson-Guptill Publications (USA), 1981.

Computer Typesetting

1 FILE NOTES

Background and concept

The increase in computer ownership and the easy availability of DTP – desktop publishing – programs ought to have led to a shrinking market for computer typesetting services. In fact the reverse is true.

Designers, even beginners just exploring the potential of their computer's Aldus PageMaker, Adobe Illustrator or QuarkXpress programs, want to design, not type text, and may choose to pay someone else, such as yourself, to input the words which they can incorporate into their design.

All the traditional buyers of typesetting services remain; notably, book and report publishers, designers, advertising agencies, printers and specialist typesetting companies who rely, at least in part, on freelance outworkers to cater for the needs of their clients.

Is this business right for you?

Only accomplished typists should consider this one. Existing computer ability, or a willingness to become thoroughly computer literate, is essential.

You'll need to understand printer's marks, how to shape a page of text, choose appropriate typefaces and learn how to produce usable pages of copy. You may need to learn how to insert the codes that operate typesetting equipment. For help with this aspect, apply direct to the makers of the equipment.

They can provide manuals, probably for a fee, and may even be able to enrol you on a special course. Alternatively, there are print courses held at various colleges.

The London College of Printing, at the Elephant & Castle in south London, is the best known of these. Look also in the media appointments section of the quality newspapers. After the job advertisements you often find small ads for computer courses. It's often a good idea to ask to see a sample part of a session from the course to check if it's right for you.

A lot of software now comes with a spell-checking facility, but grammar, punctuation and style are still beyond the grasp of most PCs. If this is something you are good at, or can bone up on, so much the better.

Not only will you be able to 'clean up' a client's copy, for which they'll be grateful, but you can also offer this as an extra editing service – for extra money.

2 DOING THE BUSINESS

As a typesetter you can work on a full-length book manu-script one minute, and turn to a letterhead or a business card the next. Typesetting colleagues of mine find ready money tapping out newsletter copy, menus, price lists, brochures, leaflets, posters, handbills and advertisements.

Typesetting books may not be furiously well paid, but the sheer scale of the project – novels are rarely less than 40,000 words, non-fiction works run to at least 60,000 words as a rule – turns book work into 'meaty' bills.

The book printer needs copy which has been prepared by being coded, in such a way that the codes tell the computer how the page should be set up (designed), which font (type-faces) to use, what point size (how big the type should be), how large the page, type area, white margins should be and so on.

Alternatively, the page can be completely input – text, style and layout specifications typed and coded in – and designed on screen, by you, or finished off by a designer – which is why designers are a useful source of work for typesetters.

The text and the commands that create the 'look' of the typeface and the layout are held on disk. You can pass the disk direct to the end user, the printer, in the book publishing example.

Usually the printer will need to have the information 'run out' to film or bromide. It is the screened film or the bromide (also known as a photo-mechanical transfer – PMT) that makes the 'plate', which is inked and which creates the printed image on the printer's paper.

Disks carrying all this information from your computer will function in compatible computers the world over. You can send your disks to the printer or designer, or you can use a modem to relay the information electronically, via special phone lines, accessible through your own phone.

3 HOW TO MARKET YOUR SERVICE

If you're aiming to work with designers or printers, you'll have to ask the right people the right questions. Can your computer 'talk' to theirs via a modem? Do they work with freelancers? Can they handle work in floppy disk form? What is their turnaround time for work? What computer language do they favour? What scale of work do they offer out? What do they pay?

Some typesetting companies employing freelance outworkers pay for work by the inch; others will pay you for how many characters you 'stroke' – key in. You'll also need to contact other people doing your type of work and resort to minor subterfuge, by, say, pretending to be an author looking for a typesetting service, in order to discover what the going rate is.

Try a similar ploy at a higher level. This time pose as a businessperson with a company report that needs typesetting;

invariably, there's one rate for corporate clients and another for private customers. Follow suit with your own tariff.

Get people in a similar line of business to send you their self-publicity material. Discover how they market themselves, what they offer in the way of bulk discounts, choice of type-faces and type sizes, what they charge for 'wanted yesterday' work and so on.

How should you charge for your services: on a project or time basis? These days clients prefer to know in advance what the bottom line will be. You might opt for an hourly rate only when working in unfamiliar keying-in territory.

When you're starting out, it pays to 'play the field', to contact every possible source of work and income, and then to whittle down the possibilities, in line with your own priorities. The biggest firms pay the most, but they may also be the slowest payers. Small firms may pay faster, but be less likely to stay in business when the going gets tough. *Yellow Pages* are a great place to start. Scan the pages under the headings 'Typesetting' and 'Printing'.

Be sure to extract all the technical information you may need: what kind and size of disks are acceptable; what type-setting machinery is used and what the codes are; what type of modem is necessary and so on.

As well as advertising in newspapers, business journals, and house organs of professional and trade organisations, consider taking display space in *Yellow Pages*, in spite of the considerable cost. Business users, searching through *Yellow Pages* in a hurry, may omit the listings and turn to the companies with enough clout or self-worth to buy display space (display advertisers get a free listing anyway).

When you advertise to the consumer who doesn't know your name, you are what you seem. A good designer and a skilled copywriter can create a winning commercial 'person-ality' for your advertisement. The same image-first thinking applies to the quality of the design, the weight of the paper and the message your headed stationery relays to prospective clients.

Your advertising copy and the sales letters you mail direct

to company 'decision makers' should emphasise all the important aspects of your service: that it is competitively priced, fast, reliable and high quality.

Some businesses find they fare much better using a direct approach, targeting their prospects precisely, using lists they hire or buy, or building their own.

A typical mailing 'package' may include a sales letter, the most important element; a brochure or leaflet outlining the scope of services on offer; price list; samples of work; testimonials (copies of letters from satisfied clients, or extracts from such letters); a reply device, such as a postcard or self-seal envelope with order form or questionnaire printed on the inside.

HELPFUL READING

Advertising Agency and Studio Skills, Tom Cardamone, Watson-Guptill Publications (USA), 1959.

A Manual on Lettering and Lay-out, L. A. Doust, Frederick Warne & Co., 1934.

A Print Buyer's Handbook, Alan Delgado, Wolfe, 1974.

Editing for Print, Geoffrey Rogers, Quarto Publishing, 1985.

Methods of Book Design, Hugh Williamson, Oxford University Press, 1956.

Preparing Art and Camera Copy for Printing, Henry C. Latimer, McGraw-Hill Book Company (USA), 1977.

Printing, P. C. M. Lamb, Robert Hale, 1967.

Technical Terms of the Printing Industry, Rudolf Hostettler, published by Rudolf Hostettler, 1949.

The Design Concept, Allen Hurlburt, Watson-Guptill Publications (USA), 1981.

Used Computer Broker

1 FILE NOTES

Background and concept

Are you a computer buff? Here's your opportunity to think laterally and turn your hobby into a money-making business. Although you are involved in the buying and selling of hardware and software, you carry no stock. Your forte is putting buyers and sellers in touch with each other. Your overheads are low, your investment nominal and the risks minimal.

Your aim is to establish a network of sellers and buyers, ideally using your computer's database facility, and you receive a fee for introducing buyers and sellers. Your unique agency position enables you to earn money from both parties.

Today, many more people are 'in the market' for computers; from students to journalists, dentists and doctors, to children and their galaxy of computer games. Almost everyone involved in communication, learning, sales and businesses of every type, now appreciates that they can no longer just 'make do' with card indexes, a Filofax and a typewriter.

To cater to the demand, computer and software companies are hard at it, building faster working processors and more manageable mice, to create the curious phenomenon we witness with virtually every consumer product: built-in obsolescence. Indeed, *The Times* says the laptop market

reinvents itself every six months! People become disenchant-
ed with their current equipment and yearn to 'trade up', as
economically as possible, which is where a service such as
yours comes in.

Not surprisingly, much of the second-hand gear coming on
the market has seen only light use, so buying used is not only
a cheaper option, it's also a relatively safe one for the buyer –
and for you. Customer satisfaction is unlikely to be a problem.

Is this business right for you?

This particular business opportunity is essentially one for the
aficionado. You don't have to be young to appreciate and
understand computers; however, many older people do seem
to suffer hi-tech hang-ups. A computer-literate enthusiast is
simply more likely to be able to (and want to) stay *au fait*
with the latest developments. Glance through magazines
such as *XYZ*, *MACWORLD* or *MacUser*, and you'll see just
how rumbustious this world can be!

Other essentials are an understanding of market forces –
the ability to talk to people in a convincing, professional way
– and a feel for costing and marketing a service. Your key to
success isn't 'buffery', however, but a helpful, questing men-
tality that addresses the real problem, best summed up by the
question: 'What do you want your computer to do?'

The Japanese built their industrial reputation on the ability
to frame the right question. If you want the right answers,
they say, you have to ask the right questions. Your task is
uncovering needs and finding solutions to problems.

2 DOING THE BUSINESS

In-depth reading of computer magazines will be just the start
of your research. When new products are announced you'll

locate stockists, telephone, sounding like a genuine prospect, and book an appointment with an able technical person who can show how the gadget works and relates to other equipment already on the market.

Only by handling hardware can you discover, for example, such things as the inherent problems of many portable laptop computers when it comes to fast typing or wordprocessing.

You'd think the laptop was the ideal freelance journalist's 'tool', just the job for the roving reporter to cart around on assignments, to take into the pub or the train. But instead, some writers (especially those who do not touch-type) find the compact laptop keyboard too cramped, since all the command keys share the limited keyboard space with the QWERTY keys.

With a desktop wordprocessor, often the command keys are separate and the QWERTY keys may even be bigger. Apple Powerbooks, Toshiba and AST laptops can all be tricky for the fast typist, whereas the Compaq Contura (on which the manuscript for this book is being written) may be a better bet.

Then again, the battery power of laptops may be overestimated, especially if you are running Windows and other power-sapping programs. Inside information like this will impress prospects and clients, and also be genuinely helpful to them.

How much should you charge for your services? That depends on your perception of what the market will stomach in terms of brokerage fees, and the size of the items or systems about which you are handling information.

There's nothing new about the notion of the fee being linked to the size of the sale. Employment agencies link their fees to the employment package offered to candidates they introduce. When you sell your home, the estate agent charges a percentage fee based on the selling price. They'll probably also vary that percentage across a band of prices, so the higher the selling price, the lower the percentage.

People dislike the idea of a brokerage fee climbing in a never-ending spiral. Happy to pay 3 per cent on a £60,000 house sale, a brokerage/agency fee of £1,800, clients may balk at paying a 3 per cent fee of £7,500 on a sale of £250,000. Somehow, seven and a half grand just feels too much.

You have to live in the real world, and the real world isn't rational, not for estate agents, and not for used computer brokers! So consider 'capping' your commission at a user-friendly level.

Here are some of the costs you'll need to take into account:

- software and hardware, purchase/lease and set-up costs;
- possible personal training costs;
- advertising;
- time spent compiling and printing questionnaires, creating and art directing advertising (never let a printer design your ad and always direct your designer);
- time spent on the phone 'wooing' prospects, taking orders for goods wanted and marketing/advertising instructions in respect of goods for sale;
- your time spent inputting and collating information;
- computer time matching buyers with sellers;
- post;
- phone;
- heat, light, rent and rates;
- letterheads and other stationery;
- travel to printer, designer and post office;
- newspapers and magazines;
- designer fees.

You'll need to design a simple questionnaire to 'map' your seller and buyer clients. Typically, this could include the following information.

> Name
> Address
> Home and work phone numbers
> Buyer/seller
> Type of computer wanted/problem to be solved
> Type of computer/etc. for sale, including:
> > make
> > model

> features, peripherals
> When bought
> Purchase price
> Condition of equipment
> Why are you selling
> Price being asked/price you are willing to pay

You can get people who phone you to respond to this questionnaire on the spot. Or you can feature the questionnaire, in an abbreviated form, in your advertisements.

Your database will enable you to file information under a number of categories. Say a customer is searching for a particular make of computer, you can ask your database to list (and print out, if you wish) all the computers you have at your disposal of that make. You could do the same with computer memory capacity or size of monitor screen, or printers able to take tractor feed paper, or print labels or run at a certain speed, and of course the client's price constraints will feature.

3 HOW TO MARKET YOUR SERVICE

Here are three ways of handling your 'for sale' information:

1. make yourself known and have people phone you for information on what you have available;
2. compile a list of items for sale and publish it, updated on a weekly or other regular basis;
3. take space in a well-liked, much-used advertising medium and list your for sale goodies, with prices or a price guide.

These are the principal ways of getting your service, and lists of client wants and 'for sales' known and circulating.

You can advertise, using classified advertisements. Here you don't have much room to manoeuvre, partly because classified advertising is relatively expensive and partly because long ads don't work so well in the classified or listing columns of a newspaper or magazine. You have to hit hard and fast.

Your ad will need to relate to a reader's own interests, pushing all the buttons that make people buy. People respond to saving money, to the word FREE (your list is distributed free), to the notion that by not acting quickly or at all they might be missing out on something. A typical classified ad might read:

LOOKING TO BUY OR SELL A COMPUTER?

Save time and money with The Computer Broker. I target buyers and sellers, saving you valuable time and money! I list your computer for less than you'd pay to run your own ad. Send for **FREE** sample list and full details. No obligation, no follow-up calls. Write **NOW** to . . . or phone . . .

This same copy might be the backbone of your display ad. With the extra space you buy you can also feature your list of items for sale and client wants. Another effective type of display ad is where you run your 'body copy' similar to the above, perhaps with an illustration, or testimonials – extracts from letters you've received from satisfied clients. And you include a coupon so people can fill it in and send off for their free list and further information. Consider offering a FREE-POST facility; you will only profit from it.

Make it easy for people to do business with you every step of the way, including paying for your service. Explore the possibility of accepting credit and charge cards. The percentage rates the card companies levy are getting lower all the time, as they thrash about for business in an increasingly competitive market.

Another tack is to advertise for buyers and sellers separately. A rule of advertising is that you get a better response with a simple message. But this is something you can 'pilot' test for yourself.

Check the response from ads that 'woo' buyers and sellers, and the response from ads that target them individually. Here's an ad designed to pick up interest only from computer buyers looking for second-hand goods:

BETTER USED COMPUTERS listed by The Computer Broker. Phone NOW for up-to-date list and prices. Tel . . . Or write . . .

Where you have a particularly exciting selection of equipment you might even feature one item large in an ad, on the basis that you draw the eye; then add facts about your own brokerage service and ability to target such interesting items.

There are other ways to market your services, such as through leaflets delivered to appropriate businesses or even left under the windscreen wipers of delegates' cars at a computer conference or exhibition. It's a downmarket technique, but it works!

Consider also raising your profile by running a seminar or workshop. Target the local business community using ads in trade and local papers and business newsletters, such as those issued by chambers of commerce. Since your event is newsworthy, announce the date and details to your local paper's news editor in a letter or press release. Enclose a professional-looking portrait of yourself (colour or black and white, postcard size at least). You could gain some useful free publicity.

You might even contemplate publishing your own mini computer price guide, perhaps with a title such as *The Insider's Guide to Second-hand Computers*. The book can be economically run out on a laser printer and comb bound. Sell it for a few pounds per copy, via your own advertisements and mailings.

Remember that your aim is to earn from both buyers and sellers. When people contact you with goods to sell, you collect a fee for featuring their items. However, you are in the position of an advertising department of a newspaper or magazine. You don't guarantee sales, you merely promise 'exposure'. Whether people respond or buy or not is in the lap of the gods. This should discourage you from ever becoming party to a 'no sale, no fee' arrangement.

When your list goes out to prospective purchaser clients (either directly through a request for the list from a coupon ad, or the list gets printed as part of an ad in a computer, or business publication or local newspaper) again you collect a fee for 'mating' buyer with seller.

As well as broking sales, you can just as easily handle swops; and if business is good, you might even consider selling cut-price new stock that you have sourced, preferably on a sale or return basis. If things go well you might even consider including featuring the services of programmers, systems people, people who repair and service hardware, and so on.

Why not? Lots of people, those running businesses especially, find a piece of software is almost right but could be fine-tuned to be exactly right for their line of work. Many software packages do allow for this 'tweaking' process. But who's got the time, the patience or the confidence? And of course you take a fee for introducing business to the service provider and also from the client requesting the service.

HELPFUL READING

So You Want to Buy a Word Processor, Helen Harris and Ela Chauhan, Business Books, 1982.

The Myth of the Micro, Rodney Dale and Ian Williamson, Star Books, 1980.

The Personal Computer Handbook, Peter Rodwell, Dorling Kindersley, 1983.

Data Management

1 FILE NOTES

Background and concept

The one thing that most people know about computers is that they're great 'dustbins' for information. You can log and file facts in a computer, in much the same way that you might make diary notes or list names and addresses and phone numbers in a Filofax or card index.

Businesses have other information to store and retrieve, such as stock levels, customer accounts, staff pay details and so on. Using the framework of a database allows you to input and arrange information in a structured way so the computer can manipulate it according to need.

This intelligent filing of information is known as database management. There's money to be made from database management, even at a basic level, which can be marketed to small, low-tech businesses who haven't either the computer hardware or the skill to do it themselves.

Is this business right for you?

You need to be computer literate and own a computer (and printer) able to run a database; the more powerful the computer, the more advanced the database you should be able to run.

2 DOING THE BUSINESS

I use an AppleMac Performa 400 to run a simple database for a client who sells motorcycles. We have a number of lists, such as general bike buyers, and a separate list of Ducati bike buyers and Ducati prospects – the Italian sportsbike the dealer specialises in.

The ClarisWorks software built into my AppleMac sorts these names into alphabetical order, totals these names, and enables me quickly to find and eliminate any duplication. I can use the Claris wordprocessing facility to draft letters to bike buyers and prospects on the database, and the mailmerge feature will ensure each letter is automatically personalised when printed out.

We use our names to send out a regular newsletter, do follow-up phone calls, invite specific groups to open days at the shop, when new models arrive and to racetrack meetings, when the shop's own race-prepared Ducati bike is defending its national title in the British, European and American Race Series.

This database service involves my organisation, additionally, in copywriting, design, printing, photography, collating inserts, stuffing envelopes, stamping and dispatching letters, and more. The client pays the brute costs of the mailing (stamps, stationery, computer consumables – ribbons, paper – photocopying), and pays me a set amount per week to maintain the database and generally handle the mailings.

The database demands in this instance are very basic, of course. Businesses use databases for the whole spectrum of business functions: invoicing and credit management; cashflow projections; general accounting, including VAT and so on.

As well as working for others you might consider using your database expertise and facility to market your own 'product'. I know of one computer adept who has set up a database on hire purchase, leasing, service and maintenance deals. Businesspeople are scared stiff of stumbling into poor office equipment leasing deals after the horror stories of the past few years. They'll pay good money for a reliable instant source of safe deals.

Then there's the man who earns a living delivering press fleet cars to motoring correspondents, and a good second income as a travel agent, using his computer to track the cheapest air-fare tickets.

I read in *The Sunday Times* supplement on the Windows Show '94, an exhibition at Olympia, that:

> American Airlines led the way in the trade business when it produced a graphical interface [point and click the mouse system] for its airline reservation system, Sabre.
>
> Now anybody subscribing to CompuServe can hook into the millions of fares from most of the world's airlines stored on Sabre, find the cheapest ticket and book it on the spot.

Another way to make money from database information is to hire out lists of prospects. A mailing list rental service is a great way to make extra income. But never give out the names of private client customers to other business operators: confidentiality is the name of the game.

Be advised that inputting computer information can be amazingly boring. Stuffing envelopes is even more tedious. So much so, in fact, that the brain makes idiotic mistakes with collating just to create some kind of variety! So you need to check constantly, at random, to see you are getting your contents right. Or farm this aspect of your business out to someone who is more amenable to dull repetitive work or needs the money more!

Mind you, the inputting drudgery is likely to lift, once the initial wadge of historical customer information has been input. Maintaining and 'cleaning' a database – monitoring for duplication of names, and adding new names – is much lighter work.

Here's a businesslike insider tip you might like to ponder. Find out what computer system your client runs. If it's a

DOS-based system, set up your database on an AppleMac system, and vice versa. The free exchange of information between rival computer companies' machines is on the cards, and already exists in certain departments, but it is not yet as easy as it should be.

Since you don't want it to be convenient for the client suddenly to decide to run the company database in-house, or hand it to some other database manager, why not cut yourself a winning hand early on in the game? You know what they say: never give a sucker an even break . . .

If you are holding customer details on computer you will need to contact and probably register with the Data Protection Registrar. Registration lasts for three years.

3 HOW TO MARKET YOUR SERVICE

You'd be surprised how sloppy some businesses are about keeping customer information; they haven't yet cottoned on to the fact that this is solid gold stuff, that it's 12 times easier to sell to an existing customer than to a new one! You can use this point to sell your service.

Businesses who use their own customer base for marketing quickly become sold on the idea. Not only do they discover easier sales, but their advertising costs drop dramatically, as (with your help) they explore more subtle and quantifiable methods of marketing.

The best way to put word around about your service is to write to managing directors of companies, using a smart letterhead and a benefit-packed letter. No businessperson is bothered about your expertise, or the cost or sophistication of your computer equipment, provided it will do the job.

They want to hear that you can save them time, trouble and money. Relate any special flexibility of your systems directly to the company's own products; spell out how creative marketing can result. Very simply, if you can show a company how to save or make more money than they are being asked to pay you, you have a good chance of securing work.

If you have a special interest or expertise in a particular field, such as chemicals, cosmetics or farming, find which trade and professional publications practitioners read, and advertise in the classified pages. You'll need to offer enquirers a simple (free) leaflet outlining your services and a price list. If that works, book a series of ads. Also consider leaflet insertions to gain the highest profile among the readership.

HELPFUL READING

How to Make Money with a Home Computer, John Lawson Neale, A.C.I.S., Carnell (DTP Report), 1991.

USEFUL ADDRESSES

Data Protection Registrar, WycliffeHouse, Water Lane, Wilmslow, Cheshire SK9 5AF (Tel. 0625 535777).

SALES AND MARKETING

Market Researcher

1 FILE NOTES

Background and concept

Market researchers are familiar figures. You find them loitering with intent in shopping malls and market squares, clipboard in crook of arm, earnest expression on face. 'Excuse me, would you mind answering a few questions on . . .'. They ring at the door to a welcome similar to that offered to Jehovah's Witnesses. Alternatively, they're ushered in with a smile of relief, God's gift to old folk or housebound mums, anxious for a bit of 'life', an unfamiliar face, and an opportunity to use the pot rather than solo tea bags.

What are they doing? Generally, they are making it easier for people to sell you things, via advertising, promotion, 'positioning' in the marketplace, and so on, occasionally uncovering information that, when translated into merchandise, really does improve your 'quality of life'. This writer believes that one of a consumer's best safeguards is the manufacturer with a reputation to lose. To gain that, in today's media-marooned society, you need a high profile and that means plenty of advertising.

When you see an advertisement in the papers or on television, it's usually the first public sign of a long marketing process that begins with a manufacturer taking the expensive decision to find out why people really buy the company's goods, or how best to present (sell) a new product or product range, or alter or improve an existing one.

It falls to the market research (MR) firm to ascertain what

the client needs to know, what questions need to be asked, of whom (by whom – which is where the market research interviewer comes in), how the information should be taken down, organised and processed.

The manufacturer then shapes its marketing strategy around what people have shown they like about the product, such as its name, packaging, advertising etc., editing out perceived dislikes, negative aspects and so on.

Market research, at the most senior levels, is a highly skilled, highly paid occupation – over £1,000 an evening for a trained psychologist managing an invited group session of respondents is not unknown. Analysing the results of a survey may take advanced statistical and computer expertise. But the information could be gathered by someone like you.

Is this business right for you?

Aptitude in an MR interviewer is a many-splendoured thing. It starts with the feet: if you don't enjoy rude health, standing, walking, climbing stairs or bad weather, turn the page. Incidentally, a car is a must in the suburbs or rural districts, though you may just about manage with public transport in a major town.

A good interviewer is a dab hand at buttonholing people who may have little time and no interest in your work or the product (which is generally not revealed until deep into the interview, if at all). Skill in talking to people, knowing how to get them to open up (more on this later), is a bonus; but never lose sight of the fact that a reliable hack, who fulfils interview quotas on time, is a more valuable person to MR companies (whose surveys always seem to be urgent) than a gifted interviewer who lacks persistence or discipline.

You don't need a degree, higher education or a BBC accent to make it as an MR interviewer or 'field worker'. Personal qualities, such as tact, integrity, affability, slow temper and a poker face, rate more highly.

You may have to work evenings and weekends, and almost certainly will have to be ready to work at short notice. Given how much long-focus strategic planning goes into MR campaigns it's extraordinary that so much of the dog soldier's work has to be done at a canter!

2 DOING THE BUSINESS

You'll probably start out by being assessed for the job with a face-to-face interview. A day or two's training, round a table with other novices, is generally followed by street trials when you either go the rounds watching your supervisor target, proposition and interview respondents, or the supervisor oversees your approach and interview techniques, and comments constructively, later, in private.

Most interviews are intricately, purposefully structured. The real skill lies in marching to orders, drawing out answers in a totally neutral way and writing (clearly, by hand) in an uncoloured style; psychoanalysing your respondents is not the name of this game. In-depth interviews – the cream of the crop for the ordinary interviewer, and not normally available without serious experience under your belt – are, however, more free-ranging and last up to two hours, with enhanced pay to match.

There are a number of levels of interviewing, in terms of depth, intensity, numbers of respondents being interviewed and interplay between respondents. The Group Interview is usually managed by a trained psychologist or moderator. Ten to twelve people attend on average; if less than six arrive the session is called off. Audio-tape or even video may be used, with permission.

Host or hostessing is another type of group interview. A hotel may be booked, and the interviews take place with respondents seated in a circle around a coffee table. Hall interviews are held in a shopping mall or marketplace. The aim is to stop passing shoppers and interview them as they stand, or take them to a convenient coffee bar and run through the questionnaire.

There are random consumer surveys, with respondents drawn from the electoral roll, or quota surveys (more common) where you must find respondents in specific socio-economic categories.

MR is largely a 'numbers game': if you go about your business in a consistent way and keep going long enough, you'll complete your quota. In one survey, having picked an apparently suitable street (right sort of car, style of net curtain, etc.), we were told to leave a gap of five doors after each interview.

It's this aspect of MR – traipsing round streets, knocking on doors and persuading total strangers to sacrifice up to an hour of their time – that floors many aspirants: as many as half don't even make it past the training stage!

One of the best jobs to come my way was posing as a 'user-chooser' in a car dealership survey. I pretended to be an executive able to choose a new company car to a certain level of price and trim. My hidden agenda was rating the salespeople in terms of helpfulness, product knowledge, etc., and the showroom according to cleanliness, display of cars, welcoming atmosphere and so on.

One cold, wet Friday evening in a Suffolk market town, a salesman, anxious to clock off for the day, passed me the keys to test drive a brand new £14,000 motor without requesting ID – not even a driving licence!

3 HOW TO MARKET YOUR SERVICE

Keep your eyes open for advertisements appearing locally, since they may well be a good source of continuing work, organised by a supervisor working regularly in your area. I responded to one such ad which read:

MARKET RESEARCH INTERVIEWERS

Agency requires local part-time interviewers in the Norwich area.

Previous experience desirable, but not essential.

Full training given.

Tel. . . .

The Market Research Society issues a list of Organisations and Individuals Providing Market Research Services (the MRS Code of Conduct booklet is essential reading). Write a letter to the managing director of each likely company, offering your services.

HELPFUL READING

Interviewers Manual, Albermarle Marketing Research, 18 Dartmouth Street, London SW1H 9BL (Tel. 071-222 2191/5).

USEFUL ADDRESSES

The Market Research Society, 15 Northborough Street, London EC1V 0AH (Tel. 071-490 4911).

Abacus Research, Eden House, River Way, Uckfield, Sussex TN22 1SL (Tel. 0825 761788).

Carrick James Market Research, 20 Seymour Mews, London W1H 9PF (Tel. 071-935 5920).

Import/Export Agent

1 FILE NOTES

Background and concept

If the prospect of trading across international boundaries, with minimal outlay and financial exposure, stirs your entrepreneurial spirit, this could be the home business for you.

Be clear about one thing: this is a kitchen table or desktop business; globe trotting doesn't enter into it, nor do you need to know foreign languages. English is the international language of trade and has been for years. But that's not to say it won't help to understand French or German, and you may find visiting key international trade fairs – some of the most important are held in Frankfurt – a prime source of new ideas and an opportunity to 'press the flesh' of people who may turn into useful trading contacts.

International trade is an obvious growth area, with a new focus of interest centred on Europe, following the collapse of the Berlin wall, the reorganisation of the former Soviet Union into independent nation-states and the establishment of single market Europe.

Trade is getting even more promising in the Far East, as Singapore and Hong Kong, Japan's former sources of cheap labour, establish their own trading empires. Chinese-run Hong Kong, now just a few years away, and a newly acceptable South Africa, are sure to provide other fresh trading opportunities.

International trade is an open book. Some 750,000 manufacturing businesses worldwide do not export, but would surely like to; and even in the USA only 10 per cent of firms export, leaving perhaps a quarter of a million companies who might welcome your approach.

An import-export agent doesn't buy or sell goods, but acts as a go-between, introducing buyer to seller, or seller to buyer. For this service you will receive a commission, based on the value of the deal. The commission can be anything between 2.5 to 15 per cent, and typically amounts to 10 per cent, all this before shipping and handling costs are counted in. Traditionally, the agent receives commission from both seller and buyer. Best of all, you stand to earn not only on the initial introduction but also on all repeat orders.

Since shipping is uneconomical unless the items are packaged in bulk, orders running into four-figure or even six-figure sums are not uncommon. Manufacturers warm to commission-only agents deals. Making new sales in unfamiliar territories might involve costly advertising campaigns, taking on extra staff or devoting precious executive time.

Where you act for the benefit of a manufacturer in your home country, finding a foreign client-buyer, you operate as an export agent. Where you act for a manufacturer in a foreign country, organising a sale in your own country, or a third country, you then acquire import agent status.

Is this business right for you?

You do not need a smart office in a central big city location. It is possible to set up an import-export business very economically. You need a desk, phone, a wordprocessor, preferably a computer with a hard disk and floppy disk facility, and a fax machine. Basic fax machines can now be bought new for under £300. But consider the better machines, such as those that use plain paper, not the shiny paper-in-a-roll that can fade in sunlight in a matter of days, and will even fade after a year, or less, when kept in a folder in a drawer – not a recipe for confident long-term business!

These more advanced fax machines can be a lot more expensive, and you should explore the possibility of economic rental or lease-purchase. You will also need to fund self-promotion, via professionally printed stationery and well-targeted advertising in low-cost trading magazines.

You'll need to study in depth the many trade magazines featuring product lines that could provide your trading stock. Basic secretarial skills are a must, also good organisation and the ability to write crisp, jargon-free enquiry letters. Consider another kitchen table business if you are daunted by 'officialese' and small print.

2 DOING THE BUSINESS

In this business, the clients are called principals, you are the agent, although you are your own boss and are never employed by either buyer or seller. The working document that you are party to with a principal is known as an agency agreement. You can piece together the information from the various trading organisations listed below. Or you can subscribe to one of several import-export agency courses.

Probably the best-known courses are those offered by Wade World Trade, established in 1946 and now with 12 offices worldwide and clients in 120 countries (see below). Easy-to-follow and well-presented course sessions include: selecting the right product; securing an agency; finding your market and making sales; terms of trade and transportation methods; payment for goods; how to negotiate and draft agency agreements. Complete courses start at just over £100 and include a free advice bureau (Wade World Trade Advisory Service) and subscription to *World Trade Digest*, brimful of advertisers offering products or seeking agency territories.

Start establishing trade links with countries where English is the main language, an official second tongue or very commonly spoken. Examples are Eire, the USA, Canada,

Australia, New Zealand, South Africa, Luxembourg, Scandinavia and The Netherlands.

You may be familiar with certain countries through your travels, ethnic origins, work or even hobby interests. For example, an antique dealer with a knowledge of the carpet trade may well be comfortable with Turkish transactions.

Countries that are not in the heartland of Europe, such as Italy, Portugal and Spain, merit the attention of world trade agents. Consider also the so-called 'North European Golden Triangle', an area bounded by Paris, Hamburg and Liverpool, roughly the size of the UK, yet containing some 60 per cent of the population of the European Union!

Your early deals might also best be set up with established economies controlled by stable governments and with strong currencies, such as Deutschmarks, dollars, yen and sterling.

Stick to goods that are unlikely to cause you headaches with the authorities or those that are already sold in quantity. Consider cut-price items that you can shift in bulk, and also high-price items you can trade in small quantities but with a high mark-up. In either case, your commission earnings will be worth while.

It's always tempting to try to be different, and it's true that your biggest successes may come with the real humdinger novelty that no one has yet seen, and you're the first to market it. The greatest challenge is launching a new product into virgin territory; it also carries the highest risk of failure.

Focus on tried and tested items, such as gifts, crafts, novelties, decorative objects, light furniture, such as bamboo and wickerwork, fabrics, clothing, jewellery and photographic equipment, manufactured to international standards.

Successful businesses include a woman who makes a comfortable living importing knitting needles, a Surrey housewife sending sportswear to Sweden and Denmark, a Thai agent exporting handicrafts and ceramics to Europe and North America, a Liverpool agent who handles antique sales to French collectors, decorators and investors, and a doctor in the north of England who imports wine to supplement his practice earnings (as well as improving the standard of his own drinking!).

Be aware of potential danger areas. The Far East yields many appealing toy lines, but regulations affecting toys are strict in the UK. Manuals on self-defence and combat, widely available in the USA, are banned in the UK. Other areas to avoid are plants, perishables and electrical goods. Some lines run on slightly different voltages or currents, or are vetted according to less stringent safety practices than in the UK. For example, American-made VHS videos will not work with British televisions.

When considering a product line, ask yourself if it compares favourably with the price and quality of similar goods already available. Your verdict on this must be tempered by considerations regarding the cost of transportation and custom duties.

There are numerous magazines, trade and import-export journals where manufacturers advertise their lines, and invite inspection and offers to buy, or state they are looking for agents or distributors. Also helpful are UK chambers of commerce, the commercial sections of foreign embassies (mostly in London) and the Department of Trade and Industry (DTI). The DTI publishes various journals and leaflets, such as *Overseas Trade* (listing important trade fairs for up to two years ahead), with a *Promotions Guide* supplement.

The DTI operates a number of regional and satellite offices, in the North-east and North-west, Yorkshire and Humberside, East and West Midlands, the South-west, South-east (London), East, Scotland, Wales and Northern Ireland; contact details are available from your local chamber of commerce or main branch library.

3 How to Market Your Service

The first step is to have your own letterhead printed. This is not as straightforward as it sounds. Letters are legal documents, and have to reveal the structure – limited company, sole trader, partnership etc. – of your business as well as your trading 'personality'. Most agents operate well enough as sole traders, though you should read as much literature as you can, or subscribe to a course, to get all the aspects of your letterhead and company structure right from square one.

Having found your product/s, via specialist journals, trade directories, general/retail wholesale directories, market reports and trade associations, you can choose one of several routes to locate buyers:

1. work through trade commissioners, boards of trade, embassies, consulates and chambers of commerce;
2. sell direct to wholesalers and other major importers;
3. advertise in the business opportunities or trade columns of the local press.

The Wade World Trade courses offer in-depth advice on all aspects of marketing and self-promotion for the import/export agent.

HELPFUL READING

Export for the Small Business, Henry Deschampsneufs, Kogan Page, 1988 (2nd edn).

How to Start your Own Import and Mail-order Business Without Capital, John Trevor, Trade Guide Publications, 1965.

Importing for the Small Business, Mag Morris, Kogan Page, 1985.

Marketing Without Frontiers 2, published by Royal Mail International (12–15 Fenton Way, Basildon SS15 4BR) and updated regularly.

USEFUL ADDRESSES

British Importers Confederation, 309–315 3rd Floor, Kemp House, 152–160 City Road, London EC1V 2NP (Tel. 071-253 9421).

Central Office of Information, Hercules House, Hercules Road, London SE1 7DU (Tel. 071-928 2345).

Croner Publications Ltd, Croner House, London Road, Kingston, Surrey KT2 6SR (Tel. 081-547 3333).

Department of Trade and Industry, Excise Advice Centre, Dorset House, Stamford Street, London SE1 9PY (Tel. 071-928 3344).

HM Customs & Excise Headquarters, New King's Beam House, 22 Upper Ground, London SE1 9PJ (Tel. 071-283 8911 for advice on licences, regulations, restrictions and duties).

Wade World Trade Ltd, 50 Burnhill Road, Beckenham, Kent BR3 3LA (Tel. 081-663 3577).

Impex Consultants (Tel. 081-997 4471).

Westlink Worldwide (Tel. 031-553 7620).

Mail Order Agent

1 FILE NOTES

Background and concept

A mail order agent sells the goods of mail order companies – famous names include Freemans, Empire, Littlewoods – via catalogues that the companies produce. These are usually heavy, glossy books, the size of London telephone directories, full of beautiful colour photographs.

The traditional stock-in-trade of the catalogue company used to be clothing. Now the range has expanded to include sportswear, gardening tools, household items, toys, carpets, bedding, furniture, computers, audio-visual equipment and more.

As an agent your typical routine would be to take catalogues round to prospects for them to look through, become enchanted with the goods and, hopefully, place orders. On your return visit, you pick up the order and payment or part payment. The company delivers ordered goods to you to sort out distribution to purchasers; bulky items may be sent direct to buyers.

It's easy to see why people enjoy buying from their armchairs. It's the lazy way to shop, with no parking problems, petrol bills to get to the shops, time wasted or even money to pay up front. Depending on the company, the value of the goods and the credit standing of the client, easy credit terms are normally on offer. Credit is free and there is no discount for cash; from which you can probably conclude that prices are higher than in the high street.

You get 'nowt for nowt' in this life, and that applies as much in this business as anywhere. Free credit suggests mark-up is built in generously to take account of slow payment. Cash customers are shrewd enough these days to try their arm at negotiating discounts even with po-faced managers in carpeted department stores; therefore it's fair to assume that people who buy from catalogues need the credit as much as they hanker after the goods.

Is this business right for you?

Agenting is very much a numbers game. It works best with a large, captive, sympathetic audience. What about 'Don't do business with friends and relatives?' That adage has taken a body blow with financial services retailing; that's where you start, according to the best brains in the business, and for mail order agents it's always been the starting point.

Thereafter a wide circle of friends is a must – a popular livewire on a housing estate might make a good go of this type of business, or someone active in a club or community centre. Country dwellers will find it heavy going, with high travel costs.

The companies work hard to portray their agents as jolly friendly people, whose visit is only marginally less welcome than that of the postman bearing a Pools winner's cheque. However, image is rarely a mirror to reality. In agent's mode, your visit is, after all, a loaded one; you are trying to entice people to buy, while your subsequent calls may be to collect instalments and chase slow payers, the company taking charge of persistent slow payers and defaulters. Nevertheless, a thick skin is a plus.

2 Doing the Business

Anyone with energy and determination can make a good second income as a mail order agent; turning this into a full-time earner is rather more involving, since your income is based on commission, which is generally 10 per cent if taken in cash, 12.5 per cent if you accept goods in lieu – remember you earn commission on goods you buy for your own family. In other words, you would need to dispose of £10,000 worth of merchandise a year to clear about £20 a week in commission income.

Working for a catalogue company you don't need to buy stock and there are no sales targets, so at least it's a low pressure occupation. Clearly, though, you only earn according to how active you are, how winning your personality happens to be and of course the appeal of the merchandise – which is why many agents often represent a number of companies.

Handling orders, returns, replacements and payment are part of your remit, and your own earnings and expenses (phone and postage) need to be faithfully monitored and accounted for, so organisational flair and a level head are also useful attributes.

3 HOW TO MARKET YOUR SERVICE

Goods are sent to clients (or you) on approval. Given this licence some agents order goods off their own backs and trust in their persuasive powers to sell them later. An enterprising, creative agent might operate a catalogue business along party plan lines, for instance.

Start close to home, with friends, relatives and neighbours. Always ask for recommendations – other people your customers think may be interested in your services. You'll need to keep your catalogues circulating, which means frequent visits to prospects.

Some sales are made 'off the page', but many more are clinched through the sales techniques/winning personality of the agent thumbing through the catalogue with a client over a cup of tea and a doughnut, pointing out new lines and special offers.

My business writing guru, the late Lou de Swart, an expert in mail order, pointed out that becoming a mail order agent was one way to 'school' yourself to go into mail order on your own account:

> You learn the rhythms and routine of business . . .
> discover which goods are in demand . . . and you start to
> build a list. The list is 'magic' to the mail order person.
> Everyone on the list is a prime prospect for your own
> lines should you decide to go independent.

One of the liveliest and most useful magazines for mail order agents is *Home Business*, published by Merlin Publications (address below). There are frequent articles on technique and new lines, and firms use the magazine (monthly, £2.25, at larger branches of W. H. Smith, Menzies etc.) to advertise for agents and distributors.

HELPFUL READING

The Home Business Directory of Income Opportunities, Merlin Publications Ltd, 14 Hove Business Centre, Fonthill Road, Hove, East Sussex BN3 6HA.

Profit Through the Post: How To Set Up A Successful Mail Order Business, Alison Cork, Piatkus Books, 1994.

USEFUL ADDRESSES

The Mail Order Traders' Association, 100 Old Hall Street, Liverpool L3 9TD.

The Direct Selling Association, 29 Floral Street, London WC2E 9DP (Tel. 071-497 1234).

Mail Order Agent

Catalogue companies:

Burlington, FREEPOST, P O Box 3, Bolton, Lancs.

Peter Craig, FREEPOST, P O Box 21, Bolton, Lancs.

Freemans Ltd, FREEPOST, London SW9.

Grattans, FREEPOST, Bradford, Yorks.

Great Universal Stores, FREEPOST, Manchester.

Littlewoods Home Shopping, Staley Avenue, Crosby, Liverpool L70 2TT.

Party Plan
Professional

1 FILE NOTES

Background and concept

Selling by party plan is a Beatles era money-spinner that has been given new life in the 1990s by manufacturers searching for economical, user-friendly alternative channels of distribution for their products.

These days, the high street has become a high-risk place to try to sell things, and mail order promotions, the traditional 'off-street' selling option, has itself become a crowded marketplace, not without its own crop of casualties. The party plan host, usually a hostess, in fact, largely on account of the type of products historically marketed in this way – plastic fridge and freezer containers (Tupperware), sexy underwear and nighties (Ann Summers), cosmetics (Oriflame and Avon), children's books (Usborne), health (Cambridge Health Plan) and so on – agrees to allow their home to be used for a party.

The party usually includes a display and verbal presentation of the products, their merits and benefits, and an invitation to sample the merchandise, spray on colognes and perfumes, try on clothes and so on.

The best parties (they can be day or night-time affairs) can be great fun, especially if some of the guests get into the swing of things and turn into impromptu models. The cheap entertainment value of party plan may also be a factor in its commercial growth.

The hostess may also be the organiser (or distributor), helping to compile a guest list, distribute and monitor the invitations, do some modest catering, as well as act as demonstrator, compère and order-taker.

Or the hostess may do nothing more than provide the party venue and refreshments. A fully fledged organiser or area agent of the parent company may be duty bound to arrange a set number of parties per week (working towards uprated commission or a bonus payment), though not necessarily have to hold them in the organiser's own home.

Party guests are encouraged to turn hostess and set up their own events, creating a geometrically expanding area of operations for the company.

Organisers may get a percentage of the orders, payable in cash (20 per cent is commonplace and 30 per cent not unknown), while the hostess may get a lower percentage of the take (10 to 12 per cent possibly), more often payable in kind.

There are other remuneration systems, which you would need to discover by contacting the various party plan companies listed below.

There may be room for promotion to area representative, management and so on. Or party plan may form a part of a larger networking operation, such as selling the Artistry range of cosmetics in the Amway system.

Whichever way you look at it, party plan is a lively and expanding home business opportunity.

Is this business right for you?

You need a comfortable home (rather than a show home, which might be offputting for those who live less well), plenty of seating and preferably with a choice of reception rooms, so even a small turnout looks 'busy'. Eight to ten people is considered an optimum number, so a large circle of friends would also be a boon.

More than a chatty socialising type of homebody, you will also need to shine centre-stage. Curiously, some unlikely candidates warm to this extroverted and unfamiliar role, possibly because the sales content is intentionally low key.

Most of the guests come prepared to buy something, and such pressure to purchase as there is often comes from other guests, wishing to be reassured in their own decisions, rather than from the hostess.

From the agent-organiser's viewpoint, however, the pressure to maintain a full diary of parties can be intense. To earn the equivalent of a full-time income may involve a certain amount of soul selling as well as product selling.

2 DOING THE BUSINESS

The best way to see if you might like this business is to contact a company, and go and see a party in full pelt, as a guest/observer. If you decide to go ahead, there will very likely be a live training session with a seasoned presenter/party giver, or training video, possibly with follow-up workshops, seminars and a newsletter.

After this induction period, expect refresher or intensive courses, new products training, and ongoing help, via a telephone hotline. Be sure you understand the commission or payment system down to the fine print – before you sign on any dotted line.

Sometimes organisers receive a not insubstantial 20 per cent of the take, in cash. Or the payment may come via an incentive scheme: the organiser buys goods from the company at a 'wholesale' price, sells them at a retail price and keeps the profit.

Clearly, if you don't do well, through lack of interest or poor product selection, and you have bought generously, you could end up out of pocket. Check, too, whether there are subsidiary costs you will have to bear, such as buying printed publicity, invitations embossed with the company logo, hostess gifts etc.

As well as organising and throwing parties there may be some quite involved record keeping and accounting to do. There is also money handling involved and goods ordered will be delivered to the hostess's home for collection by customers, who will need to be told, by post or phone (check who picks up the tab on this) that their goods have arrived.

Send for the leaflet on in-home selling produced by the Direct Selling Association; it contains a useful guide to accepted practices, ethics and so on. Also check that your domestic insurance contents policy will cover company goods and client cash kept on your premises.

3 How to Market Your Service

Party plan organisers advertise in shop windows or local newspapers to recruit party hostesses. Anywhere home-based people gather is a workable forum: noticeboards outside halls used for playgroups, libraries, waiting rooms, post offices and so on.

Party day offers some scope for presentation flair, but beware of going overboard with food and drink. Tea, coffee and biscuits are adequate, and never offer alcohol. If you are too generous, or your fare is too elaborate, you may put off those who might have offered to take parties in their own homes; they'll be afraid of not being able to keep up. A homemade cake or some home-baked biscuits go down well, as will fresh flowers, candlelight (for Ann Summers?) or seasonal decorations.

Position yourself centrally, and look to your organiser for tips on how to make your opening presentation in a lively, colourful way, and with humour. 'Ice-breakers', such as quizzes, competitions and raffles, all help defuse the tension.

As well as the established party plan companies (some are

listed below, while many others advertise on a regular basis in *Home Business* magazine), anyone with a suitable product – craft, clothing, health, published information – might consider setting up a party plan operation. You don't even have to make the products, so long as you can be assured of continuing supplies, at a sensible price, and you have the permission of the rights owner to market via the party plan route.

Contact as many of the companies as you can, research their distribution and payment methods, then do your own thing and may the force be with you!

HELPFUL READING

Home Business (monthly magazine), Merlin Publications Ltd, 14 Hove Business Centre, Fonthill Road, Hove BN3 6HA (Tel. 0273 888992).

How to Make your Fortune Through Network Marketing, John Bremner, Piatkus Books, 1994.

USEFUL ADDRESSES

Ann Summers, Gadoline House, 2 Godstone Road, Whyteleafe, Surrey CR3 0EA (Tel. 081-660 0102).

Avon Cosmetics Ltd, Nunn Mills Road, Northampton NN1 5PA (Tel. 0604 232425).

The Direct Selling Association, 29 Floral Street, London WC2E 9DP (Tel. 071-497 1234).

Oriflame UK Limited, Tilers Road, Kiln Farm, Milton Keynes MK11 3EH (Tel. 0908 261126).

The Tupperware Company, Chaplin House, Widewater Place, Moorhall Road, Harefield, Uxbridge UB9 6NS (Tel. 0895 826400).

Usborne Books at Home, Unit 8, Oasis Park, Eynsham, Oxon OX8 1TU (Tel. 0865 883731).

HEALTHCARE

Image/Beauty Consultant

1 FILE NOTES

Background and concept

'You never get a second chance to make a first impression' is one of those catchphrases that has caught on in a big way, just as 'clothes maketh the man' did in its sexist day.

I remember my class at school having to endure a daily shoe cleaning inspection, and being obliged to polish the undersides of our shoes, the raised portion between heel and sole, 'Because', so the teacher assured us, 'when you walk away from your job interview the boss will notice if you've neglected that bit of leather just because it doesn't show, and he'll draw the appropriate conclusions.' We were aged about seven at the time . . .

Today adults, in and out of business, are obsessed with their appearance, and rightly so, as everyone else seems to be – both with their own and with yours. How you look – your complexion, the sparkle of eyes, your clothes, deportment – reflects how you feel: a confident, alert winner; or a dull, shy loser; and shades of grey also-ran in between.

Studying the look of bright, successful people has resulted in quite an image industry whose practitioners argue, convincingly and profitably, that if you can uncover your own best 'look' you can lock on to an appropriate and successful image – go-getting, or relaxed and quietly confident – to suit your own personality.

Image consultancy can work on a private, one-to-one level, or it can be geared to the corporate world. My consultant friend tells me, 'Companies are warming more and more to the idea of seeking help from image consultants in a bid to improve the work performance of their staff. Confidence in personal image and style makes a tremendous difference to your professionalism.'

Running a style and image consultancy is certainly one way to earn a good living while spreading beauty and light as you go.

Is this business right for you?

Image consultancy seems to expand like the laying on of hands. A person – they tend to be female, but nervously ambitious executive men are increasingly using image consultants – has a 'makeover' (complete image change), following a consultation; is sold on the result and the technique or system used to achieve it, and decides to learn how to become a consultant in their own right.

The gist of this is that you need to be sure your own image is spot on before attempting to preach the gospel to others. Prior training as a hairdresser, beautician, model or fashion assistant would be useful; excellent colour sight is essential.

2 DOING THE BUSINESS

One successful consultant offers one or two-day workshops. The first workshop uncovers the colours that work best with the client's eye, hair, skin colour and personality. A course in skin care follows, with make-up, hair and nail treatments to close.

The price for the day includes a personalised colour sampler and a personal workbook. The next session shows how to make the most of clothes and accessories. The consultant works with the clothes a client already owns and enjoys wearing – 'Few people can afford a clean sweep'.

She shows how a client can adapt her wardrobe in a fresh way, with more appropriate accessories and figure flattering combinations. This session includes a wardrobe guide and workbook: people love being able to take away reference material that they can also dip into for an instant refresher course.

Read everything you can about image, personal presentation, fashion and body language. Interviewers in the recruitment industry, for example (article in *The Interviewer*, 13 May 1991), are advised to avoid pin stripes, strong perfume/aftershave, the colour black (females), loud nail polish, bracelets or earrings (males), military or college ties (males). Black is a non-approachable colour, creating a barrier which can prevent an interviewee opening up.

The right sort of image counselling can change the course of history – on advice, Margaret Thatcher changed her hair colour, lowered the tone of her voice and went on to win election after election! The modern image adviser is also a colour consultant; the American company Gloria Munde offers training in colour consultancy skills and techniques.

According to Gloria Munde colour is critical. Choose the wrong ones and you lose impact dramatically. A 'right' choice will make you look smarter and healthier. The theory dates back to a strange finding by a German painter from the Bauhaus School. Johannes Itten noticed that while certain students would paint a landscape with brown tones, others seemed to see shades of blue, and the preference was associated with the colour of their skin and eyes.

In the 1940s Californian style guru Carole Jackson turned the discovery into an image-enhancing system. She divided white skin tones into four divisions – spring, summer, autumn and winter. She went on to found the hugely successful Color Me Beautiful Organisation which now sponsors training and consultancy in 30 countries.

3 HOW TO MARKET YOUR SERVICE

Top-flight publicity material is a must. Use a professional copywriter and an even better photographer: the portrait of you smiling off the page of your sales literature has to be proof of the pudding or you're wasting your time!

Send these tasty flyers and leaflets to personnel and marketing chiefs, or managing directors, together with a personal letter outlining the benefits of image counselling and include a few choice quotes from some of your reading. Talk business to businesspeople.

They're not interested in colour theory, only in how looking right will help their salespeople or representatives make more money or be more effective ambassadors for the company. Follow through with a phone call, a few days later.

HELPFUL READING

Colour Me Beautiful, Carole Jackson, Piatkus, 1988.

Presenting Yourself: A Personal Image Guide for Men, Mary Spillane, Piatkus, 1993.

Presenting Yourself: A Personal Image Guide for Women, Mary Spillane, Piatkus, 1993.

The Complete Style Guide, Mary Spillane, Piatkus, 1991.

Personal Fitness Instructor

1 FILE NOTES

Background and concept

With a growing interest in health, keep fit, yoga, aerobics and weight training, this is the one-to-one counterpart to keep fit classes. Private instruction suits some people more than any communal activity. People are happy to pay more for an intensive, focused service and also for the cachet of boasting about one's own personal fitness trainer ...

The personal touch may be sought by those with unsociable jobs whose 'off times' don't coincide with public keep fit evening class hours or even the more flexible opening times of a private gymnasium.

Besides, some people are frankly too embarrassed to appear in public and, again, need to build confidence – usually a concomitant of improved muscle tone and return of lost figure shape – before joining other fitness fans fighting the flab.

Those who prefer to progress at their own pace, which may be slower or even faster than group pace, and can afford the higher bill, will warm to your service.

Is this business right for you?

You don't need to be young, well muscled or lovely. But you do need to be fit and well looking, on the basis that you practise what you preach and it works!

2 DOING THE BUSINESS

For safety's sake, the more training you have undergone the better. There are obvious health risks with overweight, ailing or elderly clients, and you should be sure they have been recently seen and cleared by a doctor for the exercise regime you have in mind.

Ideally you will have gained a respected fitness diploma (talk to the YMCA and your own local education authority about where and when to enrol, costs etc.); and you may also have spent time studying how to teach, how to respond to and cater for learner's needs.

Your clients may expect you to visit them at home, or they will come to you, in which case you will need to equip a room, outhouse or large garage in your own home. Provided there is good lighting, ventilation and warmth, the design details are less important.

Eventually you may want to accumulate many of the accoutrements of a regular gym: exercise bar, rowing and cycling machines, weights, step-up blocks, sound systems and so on.

You may need planning permission to run such a business from home (contact your council for their verdict on this), and you should certainly take out public liability and professional indemnity insurance.

People who go to group gymnasium sessions expect to pay a few pounds per workout. Private instruction can be charged at five or ten times the group rate, with an initial lesson for 'fitness assessment' costed higher.

3 HOW TO MARKET YOUR SERVICE

Choosing a route to fitness is part of the fun for fitness fanatics or older people just wanting to keep agile. Tai-chi is one of the more popular regimes, on account of its close association with kung-fu; one teacher describes it as an 'internal' style of kung-fu. Dance and aerobics (the 'no gain without pain' school of fitness) classes also have their *aficionados*. The more versatile you are, the more in demand your services will be.

Advertise using business cards or leaflets, wherever people go to keep fit – squash courts, swimming pools, golf clubs (I once heard it said that golf was a great sport – walking – interrupted!) and in sports shops.

Another angle you could explore involves targeting prospects when they are most aware of their failing figures: when they are out buying clothes. Consider getting the manager or manageress to let you display your (tastefully designed) leaflets on the counter. The fee could be a free course of keep fit for the manager.

USEFUL ADDRESSES

National Coaching Foundation, 114 Cardigan Road, Headingley, Leeds LS6 3BJ (Tel. 0532 744802).

Training and Development Department, London Central YMCA, 112 Great Russell Street, London WC1B 3NQ (Tel. 071-580 2989).

Recreation and Sports Studies Department, University of East London, The Barking Precinct, Longbridge Road, Dagenham, Essex RM8 2AS (Tel. 081-590 7722).

Development Officer, Keep Fit Association, Francis House, Francis Street, London SW1P 1DE (Tel. 071-233 8898).

Naturopath

1 FILE NOTES

Background and concept

Alternative medicine and alternative healing have come out of the closet, helped, no doubt, by royal approval. We are on the foothills of remarkable discoveries about the human body and mind.

Or rather, rediscoveries; much of this knowledge dates to earlier civilisations, but was lost or abandoned in the Age of Reason. Arguably, the rigid orthodoxy of two centuries has blighted science and medicine: a result of too much progress and not enough understanding, some would say.

The aim of naturopathy is to encourage the self-healing properties of the body, by providing the correct environment, both mental and physical. The naturopath uses no drugs or surgery, but aims to promote health and ease patients' stress using natural methods. The initial consultation usually involves a discussion, taking a case history and a physical examination. Treatment, which may include special diet, fasting, psychotherapy or massage, follows diagnosis.

There are many specialties in alternative medicine: homoeopath, kinesiologist, medical herbalist, osteopath and more. Naturopaths tend to work privately, sometimes attached to a group of professionals in associated disciplines, or are retained consultants to health farms.

Is this business right for you?

How many of the following personal attributes can you claim to have: intuition; insight; compassion; patience; discretion; gentleness? These tend to be the hallmarks and distinguishing features of a successful practitioner in this field.

If a home-based career in naturopathy appeals, you should investigate the various techniques and discover where you own aptitudes lie, for example in massage.

2 DOING THE BUSINESS

The tendency may be to imagine that naturopaths are gifted cure-all Houdinis who just 'get on with it'. Far from it. For practical reasons, as well as the demands of professionalism and the desire for probity, this is never the case. Aspirants to the calling (who need to enjoy good health) can attend full-time training at the British College of Naturopathy and Osteopathy; the registering body is the General Council Register of Naturopathy (GCRN).

You will need good GCSE or O level grades (at least two of which will be chosen from maths, physics or English language), and a pair of A Levels from among zoology, biology and chemistry.

Studies, which extend over four years, cover pathology, anatomy, nutrition, biology, orthopaedics, geriatrics and opthalmology. Graduates can apply for membership of the British Naturopathic Association.

One of the less well-known healing systems, sometimes associated with naturopathy is kinesiology, the study of the mechanics of bodily motion, especially muscle movements, and their relationship to our body system. Kinesiology also lends itself well to allergy testing.

The secret lies in non-invasive muscle testing – in other words, nothing is injected. Instead the kinesiologist tests strength of muscle response through reflex movements.

Other ailments that may be alleviated include migraine, irritable bowel syndrome and eczema. The system uses the meridian lines of the body and the basics can be learnt on a three-day course (see Don Harrison's address, below). You should ask your insurance broker about professional indemnity and public liability insurance.

3 How to Market Your Service

Alternative therapists are as chary of advertising their services as doctors, dentists and lawyers used to be. Only charlatans need to shout, seems to be the message.

Instead naturopaths rely on quiet word of mouth recommendations. My kinesiologist contact has been busy for years and never advertises. The GCRN publishes a register of Naturopaths available from public libraries and Citizens' Advice Bureaux. Copies are also available from The Secretary at the BNA registered office below. There is no restriction on advertising.

Helpful Reading

Acupressure, Michael Reed Gach, Piatkus Books, 1990.

Applied Kinesiology, Tom and Carole Valentine, Thorsons, 1985.

Aromatherapy, Daniele Ryman, Piatkus Books, 1991.

The Reflexology Handbook, Laura Norman with Thomas C

USEFUL ADDRESSES

The British Naturopathic Association, Frazer House, 6
Netherhall Gardens, London NW3 5RR (Tel. 071-435 8728).

CONSULTANCIES
AND
AGENCIES

Dating Bureau

1 FILE NOTES

Background and concept

Nobody would deny the need for dating and marriage bureaux. Dating agency advertisements proliferate. Almost every newspaper has its 'personal' or 'loveline' classified columns. And television has discovered the high-rating attraction of the 'mating game', with *Blind Date* and *Love Call*, an Anglia TV special in which love-lorn studio guests reveal all about themselves and then answer telephone calls from viewers who chat them up, hoping for a date.

It ought to be a relatively straightforward matter to meet prospective partners, but it clearly isn't for the many people who make use of the various dating organisations. Very many more souls must remain silently, painfully lonely without ever trying a bureau service.

As people get older, they become less inclined to take chances with strangers, go out less and meet fewer people. Our ageing population is likely to find this an increasing, not a diminishing problem.

If finding partners is a numbers game, the more people one comes into contact with, the greater the chance of meeting Mr or Miss Right. It follows that those who live in sparsely populated areas will have an even greater need for this type of service.

While city life regularly loses its appeal for those in established relationships, and those about to start or expand their families, single people ought to be enjoying the prospect of exciting chance encounters in a bustling environment. However, many find the urban singles scene fraught, daunting and uncertain.

Against this background, there is a real need for a dating service that is sympathetic, and perhaps rather less intrusive and ambitious than the traditional marriage agencies of days gone by.

Anyone who has ever been part of the singles scene, at any age, senses that there is someone out there for them, a romantic match that is totally right. The difficulty is in finding that special person. Most people may give up the search or settle for less.

Your aim is to try to partner people through their interests – probably using the vetting and matching facility of computer database software – and let romance work its magic if it will.

If the service you offer raises hope and improves the odds for happiness even slightly, you will have been worth your fee many times over.

Is this business right for you?

Do you like people? Do they respond to you? Do friends turn to you for your advice, insight, sympathy and comfort? Do strangers? Your most enduring and valuable skill in this business is the ability to relate to clients, empathise with their situation and understand their frustrations.

A lot of your work will be done over the phone. Is your voice one people warm to and trust? As much as you have a sensitive, feeling side, so you must also have the ability to be direct and forceful, where necessary, to help a client give voice to a problem and together deal with it in a practical way.

A background in personnel (can you write compelling letters?), counselling or marriage guidance is a distinct advantage, as might be some kind of psychological or statistical background. Since a disproportionate number of your clients are, for easily appreciated reasons, likely to be foreign, languages or familiarity with ethnic customs and practices would be an advantage.

Computer literacy is a must. From a practical point of view, you will need a fairly powerful computer, suitable database software and a versatile printer, probably laser or bubble jet.

2 DOING THE BUSINESS

A computer dating service is very easy to set up and run. The nub of the business is collecting information from paying clients, usually through questionnaires, and then using your computer database to match personality traits, age, religion, physical characteristics, stated personal preferences, location, status, hobbies and interests, and so on.

Questions such as: 'Do you like going to parties?' 'Do you take an interest in current affairs?' and so on, can be easily handled using the scale rating system, familiar from market research questionnaires. Here's an example, 'On a scale of 1–10, how concerned would you say you are about current affairs?'

The more you understand about why people find others attractive, the more insightful your questionnaire will be, the livelier and more relevant the questions, and the more precise the matching potential.

Your first stop is your library. Spend time looking through books on the psychology shelves, paying particular attention to anything on compatibility. Try to obtain a copy of *Psychology, The Science of Mind and Behaviour*, by Richard D. Gross which has useful material on interpersonal attraction.

After 'academic' study, move on to the marketplace. Write or call other dating services and ask to be sent their literature as if you were a prospective client. As much as you are tapping into their experience and expertise, so your aim will be to improve on their techniques to build your own business and reputation by offering an even better service.

When you have formulated your questionnaire – a maximum of 50 questions is recommended – and settled on your unique marketing personality, you'll want to advertise and promote your service to attract prospects, and establish a clientele. In the early days you may need to gather personal details of friends and relatives who are in the market for a dating service to give you practice with your database and matching facility.

3 HOW TO MARKET YOUR SERVICE

The experience of successful practitioners in this field suggests that your trading name should have an upbeat, positive and romantic ring to it, such as Love and Laughs, Power of Love, The Dating Game and so on.

Your advertising should have a professional aura, yet also be light-hearted, to overcome the anxiety some people will feel about making that first tentative move in the direction of a dating bureau.

The wide world may be cynical about your type of service; they may view resorting to a dating agency as a failure to make that crucial personal connection in the normal way, but your clients are in fact acting positively.

No one says they must stop meeting and relating to people they meet in day-to-day life. It's just that through your agency they are suddenly in close contact with numbers of putative partners. Your sales literature should relay understanding and commitment, and suggest that registering with your bureau is an intelligent, logical move.

People should be made to feel comfortable and trusting, and one of the best ways to achieve this is not to take the dating business too seriously. Life is a gamble, and so is love, and given a healthy optimism, and constitution, we can carry on playing the game till we drop!

Successful marketing strategies take account of the fact

that clients are often active users of other dating services. They've come to you because they are dissatisfied with the competition – or have exhausted the dating options they've been offered! Use this unease to blow your own trumpet.

Once you have a track record and can talk honestly about your successes, don't be slow in coming forward. When people send you gushing letters of thanks for introducing them to the loves of their lives, as they surely will, ask permission first and use these letters in your own marketing initiatives.

Better than competing with other bureaux on price, offer a more generous service. A lot of these charge by the number of contacts provided. Offer more matches for less money; your reputation will grow.

Active marketing can be a winner in the dating business. Consider having promotional leaflets printed and handing them out in busy shopping centres and malls. Insider tip: choose good-looking young men and women to give out the flyers. The suggestion is that attractive people flock to your organisation.

You can even use the flip side of the leaflet to print your questionnaire. Clients can fill it in and send you a cheque to be registered, or to receive more information over the phone.

One last point. Your clients are sensitive people, easily put off, easily embarrassed. Putting together advertising and copy in these circumstances is really a job for a professional advertising agency or a skilled copywriter.

HELPFUL READING

Psychology, The Science of Mind and Behaviour, Richard D. Gross, Hodder & Stoughton, 1992.

USEFUL ADDRESSES

Association of British Introduction Agencies, 23 Abingdon Road, London W8 6AL (Tel. 071-937 2800).

Financial Consultant

1 FILE NOTES

Background and concept

The 'financial consultant', a euphemism for a seller of life insurance and investments, gained currency in the mid-1980s, a boom time for the industry.

For a while, being a financial consultant (or an estate agent, foreign exchange dealer or commodities broker) was no shudder-making thing to be: stigmas tend to fade when there's serious money to be made.

The industry was given a thorough shake-up, with tiers of regulation, and in 1986 the Financial Services Act was passed 'to protect investors from incompetent or unscrupulous operators'.

When recession hit the UK economy the industry slumped. The gravy train ground to a halt. Its fuel, 'disposable income', had dried up.

The get-rich-quick gloss has gone, yet curiously, the stigma has never returned. Selling insurance is now a minor profession, like many another, with a stringent training programme, an improving regulatory system, complaints procedures, and modest rewards for hard work and long hours.

Collecting insurance premiums is the lower rung of the profession and may or may not be accompanied by a remit to sell insurance products.

Essential ground rules remain. Namely, it is a criminal offence to arrange investments or offer advice without being authorised. And financial advisers, as they now tend to be known, are classed either as 'wholly independent intermediaries', with the authority to sell the products of a number of companies, or as 'company representatives' or 'tied agents', authorised to sell the products of a single company.

There are two types of representative: a company representative and an introducer representative. Companies employing representatives are likely to be registered with the Personal Investment Authority (PIA).

A company representative will be trained in accordance with PIA's requirements, and is usually qualified to sell investment vehicles – endowment insurance, pension and savings plans, annuities, unit trusts, personal equity plans and so on.

An introducer can introduce customers needing advice to an authorised company representative, but not sell or advise.

Is this business right for you?

Essential attributes for a collector are numeracy, an easy manner, being a good mixer and well turned out. It helps to have an affable manner or you might find getting through the door difficult to accomplish on a regular basis!

Previous experience in a 'people' business, such as selling, exhibition work, market research, personnel or market trading, would be a distinct advantage.

Selling insurance demands all the familiar selling skills – determination, durable skin, self-assuredness, persistence. To operate from home you will need to be mobile.

2 DOING THE BUSINESS

Collecting insurance premiums is the least demanding work carried out by the home-based insurance representative, or 'field staff', as they are sometimes known. It's regular (modestly) salaried work.

More interestingly, it's the chummy, 'feet under the table' aspect of home visits that makes selling life and general insurance policies (for house contents, bricks and mortar, car, business), and possibly also investment vehicles (explained above), something of an easier pitch for the roving, home-visiting rep.

Selling anything demands a certain doggedness and impassiveness in the face of rebuttal. Typically it's the constant rejection that floors many would-be insurance sellers.

Insurance people, and salespeople generally, know that it's a numbers game; 'most deals don't make', is a favourite and inarguably true expression beloved of the American sales gurus. In plain language, this means if you present a proven-effective proposition to enough well-chosen prospects you must make headway – and sales.

Not surprisingly, money motivation is a prime factor for the insurance seller: the commission rewards on life and investment sales can be considerable.

To get started, contact big name insurance companies. Read their copious literature and get accepted on to their training programme.

You'll need a clean driving licence, no criminal record and reasonable health: a friend of mine with mild asthma was turned down by one company.

After that, there is a lot of movement within the industry, in pursuit of higher remuneration and a not inconsiderable number of perks, such as low interest mortgages, car purchase loans, cheaper vehicle and home insurance, share option schemes, private health plans and more.

3 HOW TO MARKET YOUR SERVICE

The most successful insurance sellers ignore the adage, 'Don't do business with friends and relatives.' They start close to home and progress from there. If you aren't sold on your company's products, why should anyone else be? And if you are sold, why not spread the good news among your nearest and dearest? That's the theory, at any rate.

Successful people in this business tend to be good mixers, with a lot of fingers in a lot of pies. You should join local clubs, such as Rotary, golf, Lions, sports clubs – anywhere business and professional people are likely to congregate and relax.

If your home is suitably smart and/or comfortable you may like to follow the story of one successful insurance company of the 1980s.

The company operated a quite rigid policy of never going out to prospects (or established clients, for that matter). Instead, the customer was obliged to visit his or her personal adviser in the insurance company's offices.

Their reasoning went like this. 'We are professionals, as much as a solicitor or a doctor, whose clients visit them in their offices or surgery. We will create and foster that professional image by insisting our customers do likewise.'

As a visiting representative you may find it harder to sell to people on their own territory. Psychology apart, there is a lack of control inherent in the situation: you may find children, spouses or the telly may offer irresistible distractions in the client's home. Consider encouraging clients to visit you in your home and check for improved sales performance.

HELPFUL READING

If You Don't Mind my Asking: 33 Ways to Defuse Objections in an Interview, George Steinberger, R. & R. Newkirk (USA), 1980.

Prospecting Systems for Success, Gordon D. Hawkins, R. & R. Newkirk (USA), 1981.

Selling More Life Insurance, Herbert N. Casson, *The Efficiency Magazine* (undated).

Skills/Goods Barter Agency

1 FILE NOTES

Background and concept

In the closing years of the twentieth century, thrift, not greed, is good – good for the soul and good for business too, apparently.

In America the founders of a newsletter with the unpromising title of *Tightwad Gazette* have become fabulously rich as subscriptions have soared. Recession-hit families have leapt at the chance to learn about bulk-buying techniques, economies of scale in cooking and general cost-cutting wrinkles that save families a small fortune around the home.

The UK response to domestic hard times has been the nationwide establishment of (at the last count) 200 'LETS' (local exchange trading systems – also known as local employment and trading schemes).

The LETS idea, a barter system in which individuals in local communities exchange services or goods for a local currency, originated in Canada and came to Britain in 1991. The scheme works equally well in town or country settings.

Barter, of course, predates coinage or other currency. My own input into this esoteric marketplace has been the establishment of a newsletter (still embryonic), entitled *The Barter Bible*. The intention is to sell subscriptions locally. You could try the same idea in your own area.

More accessibly, as a LETS founder-organiser, with a desirable service to trade, you would benefit from being at the centre of things, learning first about all the services on offer. So, though you won't earn hard currency from your business interest, you might be able to get your lawn cut, house painted, kids coached or cared for, car serviced and so on, and thereby save an awful lot of money. And, as you know in business, the easiest way to make money is to save it.

Is this business right for you?

You need energy, a good sense of organisation, marketing flair, the ability to elicit information from people, and get them excited enough to become involved and act. It will help to be mobile and ownership of a vehicle with a serious carrying capacity could be a distinct advantage.

2 DOING THE BUSINESS

To set up a LETS, all you need is a group of people who agree to swop services or goods among themselves for a notional currency. In Kingston-upon-Thames, 80 members of the Beacon Environmental Centre have set up a micro-economy using the 'beak' as their favoured unit of exchange. A beak is worth about £1 and equates to ten minutes' or so's worth of work. Skills can be costed at the going rate for that type of service, or time only may come into the equation, with no distinction made between manual or 'brain' work.

On joining the Kingston group, at a fee of five beaks, new members receive a cheque book in which they can record debits and credits. Each month members receive a statement showing their account balance; those in credit are encouraged to spend their beaks.

Services, which are advertised on a noticeboard at the centre, range from hairdressing and carpentry to plumbing, caring, nutrition counselling, babysitting and massage. Parties sort out their own deals, as businesspeople do in many cases in private. One marketing person known to me says, 'I'm talking to a motorcycle dealer where a courtesy bike is part of the proposal to promote the dealership, and a restaurateur is being asked to subsidise my eating with a third off the menu price, on top of an agreed fee for publicising her restaurant.'

The chummy, parochial gloss to the LETS schemes is no accident. Though the Inland Revenue may ignore barter arrangements (if it ever gets to hear about them), as long as they remain local affairs between consenting adults, they take a more probing interest in anything that can be construed as a professional service or a bona fide business. It's not the beaks, or other tokens that concern the tax inspectors, but the actual market value of the services or goods being traded.

Those receiving Social Security benefit, such as income support, may find themselves similarly under scrutiny and risk a benefit cut if their bartering activities are classed as work that breaches the department's strictly enforced rules. This isn't so much the black economy as an ill-defined charcoal-grey one. Exponents of LETS argue that being able to operate without money gives the cash-strapped an opportunity to muster their forces and work their way back into the mainstream economy.

3 How to Market Your Service

You can drum up enthusiasm for your own LETS through small-scale advertising – shop windows cards, leafleting, mini posters in libraries, crèches, church halls and so on. However, by far the best (and cheapest) way to get a LETS off the ground is to contact the news editor of your local paper, either in person or with a brief (250 words maximum) written news story (press release).

Map out your aims, your background, the service you offer, which services you would like to encourage, any response you've had and enclose a good, crisp portrait photograph of yourself, either a colour print or black and white.

This 'on your bike' self-help movement is being given some impetus by certain enlightened councils who are making grants available towards setting up LETS; write to LETS Link UK, address below.

HELPFUL READING

500 Money Saving Ideas, Rosemary Burr, Margaret Dibben and Wendy Elkington, Rosters, 1986.

1001 Save-money Motoring Tips, Ron Naylor and Leslie Webb, William Luscombe, 1976.

How to Buy Almost Anything Secondhand, Richard Ball, Astragal Books, 1981.

The Bargain Book, Barty Phillips, Pan Books, 1982.

USEFUL ADDRESSES

LETS Link UK, 61 Woodcock Road, Warminster, Wiltshire BA12 9DH (Tel. 0985 217871).

CV Consultant

1 FILE NOTES

Background and concept

Almost every job-seeker needs a CV. You've heard the adage, 'You never get a second chance to make a first impression'. A CV is that first impression – on paper. In the wake of recession, more and more people are out there looking for jobs in a contracting market. A well-crafted and shrewdly targeted CV can be the key to work or open the door to career enhancement.

Employees respond to persuasive CVs, often because many jobs have an element of selling or marketing. If candidates can package themselves effectively, bosses may well feel they are equipped to shift the company's goods, promote the firm's services or be a credible ambassador for the business.

Over the last 10 or 15 years, the CV has developed into a much shorter, 'sexier' document, prompted by that most urgent imperative: lack of executive time. Personnel hirers, understandably, resent the chore of sifting through long, poorly targeted, unsolicited CVs. Even vetting the CVs they have requested often seems only a marginally less onerous task!

If the CV is a selling document, so too is the brief letter that should accompany every CV. The covering letter should point out, quickly, vividly, what the applicant can do for the company. If a job-hunter can demonstrate that he or she is worth more to the company than the salary expected, clinching a job is virtually assured.

Many unemployed executives will have left their jobs with a golden, or at least a pewter or brass, handshake. This helps to explain why some CV consultants charge as much as £60 for a CV. One CV service company advertising in *The Sunday Times* charges £25 for a career starter CV (for students and those approaching their first job); £40 for a standard CV (for positions below manager, or a senior or specialised appointment); and £60 for an executive CV.

These prices include laser printing on good paper, 12 copies and all corrections. Extra copies are charged at £1.50 each with initial order, £2.50 for a subsequent request, with a minimum charge of £10 for printout reorders!

There may also be 'add-on' services – such as computer disk storage of CV information, updating CVs, special stationery, binding service, drafting and printing covering letters, counselling (£225 a session with one company), image consultancy and personal presentation, interview technique training, company research (financial information etc. on targeted companies being approached) and so on.

One CV consultancy offers a telephone service. CV details are taken down over the phone. The telephone service is charged at £10 to £15 extra.

Is this business right for you?

Becoming a CV consultant isn't something you do in a vacuum. It isn't just about being able to type a neat page according to set rules, in the same way as the ability to draw doesn't mean you can become a successful cartoonist; you also have to know how to make people laugh. In the CV business you also have to understand and appreciate what employers are looking for, often with scant evidence of their wants, gleaned from a job advertisement half the size of a postcard. Therefore it pays to have recent experience of the job market, or perhaps to have been a boss, or in the position of people hirer yourself.

Counselling may be another useful skill. Not everyone who comes to you will be a go-getter. And even young people develop a kind of self-effacing lethargy when they've been out of work too long. It will be up to you to enthuse, and also draw out information about skills, achievements, aptitudes and preferences that may not be immediately forthcoming.

Last, and not least, you must expect CV prospects to call on you in your own home. Is the setting right, or could your room or work area be made to look neat enough to convince a professional that you are up to the important job in hand?

2 DOING THE BUSINESS

A CV is ideally prepared with at least one face-to-face meeting. Why? Part of the problem with self-drafted CVs is that the candidate cannot see the wood for the trees ... or plays down qualities that a knowledgeable outsider identifies as critical for success. This meeting may take you about half an hour; an unintense interview, usually with tea or coffee thrown in.

Preparing a CV will take about another half an hour of your own quiet, private time. As the client leaves, ask him or her to stand by for a phone call, usually in a few days.

Your phone call should say the CV is completed to draft stage, ready for checking and printing out. The client is also alerted to have payment ready to hand over, preferably in folding money.

The second visit is usually over in a few minutes; most clients are delighted with the draft, make few if any corrections and ask for about five or six copies to take away. This will cost them a further few pounds.

Start your CV service cautiously, with minimum financial exposure. If you don't already have the equipment described below, don't rush out and buy it. Hire it. The secret of many a successful business is testing. You can test the water with your advertising and marketing, and then invest in capital

CV

equipment only if the market is there and, importantly, you enjoy the work.

CVs need to be wordprocessed, rather than typed, since there may be corrections or last-minute thoughts to be included. If your CV assignments are stored on disk, you can earn easy money for future printouts.

A good desktop computer costs less than £600 new; shop around and you may be able to get a printer thrown in, too, at that price. The second-hand market is also worth exploring. Wordprocessing electronic typewriters aren't as good as a full-size monitor. You see less of the page and design is a bit hit and miss. Also essential are a letter-quality printer and a telephone answering machine.

Another important part of CV preparation is an advanced feel for language. I was asked to prepare a CV for an insurance salesman. He had ceased to sell insurance, owing to a revised strategy of his employer, and now did little other than collect premiums. He dearly wanted to get back into selling, with its greater prestige and bigger, commission-based pay cheques.

An insurance collector is hardly a high status insurance job, so I changed 'insurance collection' to 'territory management'. In fact all my client 'manages' is himself and his own work routine, but the high status notion of 'management' is established.

3 HOW TO MARKET YOUR SERVICE

The cheapest way to test the water is to place cards announcing your CV business in a shop window. Some of my best responses have come from free supermarket noticeboards. They let you leave cards on show for about a week. You may need to use their own specially printed 'Customer Information' cards.

The trick is to take home a handful of blank cards when

printer, not by hand; if necessary print on to plain white paper and stick this neatly on to the card. Replace with a freshly dated card every time you do the shopping. My first card looked like this:

COULD A NEW CV GET YOU A BETTER JOB?

Is your CV old fashioned . . . too long? Modern managers warm to candidates who 'cut the cackle'. I'll focus your career . . . help you get the job interviews you want. Work with Mel Lewis, business books author and self-promotion expert. CVs from £10.

Tel: Mel Lewis 0986 (Bungay) 894829.

My cards started to disappear after a few days, and I assumed the store resented my advertising a business service in what was really a 'buy and sell' section for customers. So, I gave my cards a new heading:

POWERFUL NEW CVs FOR SALE

I hoped the store would conclude that here was some shopper trying to offload a Citroën deux chevaux motor car, popularly known as a 2CV ... The assumption must have been accurate, for this time my cards stayed up!

Remember always to ask a prospect where they saw your card: this kind of easy follow-up research can save you time and money. Once you can identify shops or other advertising locations (or press media, when you come to advertise in classified columns) that pull in no, or little, business, stop using them and concentrate on outlets that do work for you.

The next step is to spread the net: to advertise in local and national newspapers and trade magazines. Most established paid-for provincial papers will have a classification for CVs or business services, probably close to the business or City pages.

If you can identify professions with a high current unemployment rate, such as architecture, you could target the profession's trade publications. Main libraries will have a *Willings* or a *Benn's* or a *Kelly's* guide; even if you cannot find a relevant trade journal, you can always phone an architect (or whoever), and ask what people in that profession read and respect. By far the best and most up-to-date publication, listing virtually every publication, is *UK Media Directory*, published by Two-Ten Communications.

Here's an important tip: you should only advertise in publications where there are already people offering a CV service. If others are already using a particular medium as a marketplace on a regular basis, presume they find it worthwhile to be there. They have done some costly research for you, so follow their lead.

You cannot copy someone else's advertisement, word for word (including mine!); that would be breach of copyright and potentially actionable in law. But you can adapt an ad and make it your own.

The first step is to monitor the competition. A cutting from a fairly recent *Sunday Times*, possibly the most prestigious advertising forum for CV services in the UK, reveals nine advertisers.

The biggest ad offers a FREEPHONE (0800) number. Readers are invited to call for an information pack, presumably also free. 'FREE' is a great word to use in any ad. However, the ad poses an important question. Is it better to sell directly 'off the page', to get prospects to send in rough note CVs, or phone to make an appointment to visit, or is it better to offer more information through the post, to let that extra information complete the selling job for you?

The answer is that it's often more profitable overall, though more expensive in terms of print and postage costs, to sell in two stages. If you can pull enquiries, you can sell at your leisure and at much greater length, using your own paper and print, at a fraction of the cost of buying advertising space.

'Skills assessment' is another benefit offered in the paper. I suspect that most *Sunday Times* readers have a pretty good idea where their strengths lie and this may be less appetising bait.

'Interview technique training' is an excellent example of a fee-enhancing add-on service. You can charge a lot more for an afternoon one-on-one, or seminar group training session with an expert, on say interview technique, than you ever could from simply hacking out a CV. Also featured are:

- laser printing;
- same day CV service;
- payment by Visa/Access.

A modern CV can mention college or further education institutions and leave out schooling altogether. What is relevant is what was *achieved* at school, college or night classes. The exception to this rule would be where the earlier school is a famous or highly rated one and, an important point, where this is likely to influence a decision-maker favourably.

The tendency with mature candidates is to leave out interests, hobbies and pastimes, unless these are especially spectacular or relevant. For example, if a man were applying for a security post, it would help, not hinder or waste time, to add that he was keen on martial arts. Here are more pointers to job-getting CVs:

1. Your client's 'story' is more interesting than his or her history. The most effective CVs are rarely chronological.
2. You'll need to 'handle' an imperfect past. The last years of the Thatcher administration were brightened by one minister's admission that he had been 'economical with the truth'. That's the right sort of approach to have with CV preparation.

I know a man of 54, a self-made businessman who sold out his electrical company to begin a comfortable, but boring retirement. The last I heard he'd landed a job as distribution manager for an engineering company. They wanted distribution experience, not a full head of hair. In his case, relatively advanced age was less of a drawback. Also, my friend 'lost' a few years on the way to the CV page.

3. Learn to enhance your client's 'EEC' quotient. It stands for:

> **Energy**
> **Enthusiasm**
> **Commitment**

4. Where the client needs a CV to respond to a specific, advertised position, ask to see the original job ad. If the client has done his or her homework and garnered background details on the company (and possibly also competitors), you'll want that too.

The point is that you are going to pull out the qualities and experience called for – in the order they are mentioned, which will be the order of importance in the hiring company's eyes – and then match up your client's skills, qualifications and experience.

In a survey, major American companies said they prefer CVs that are organised to be easy to read, with bold headings. Lots of white space also helps. Don't run text right across the page. Establish a narrower measure for your information. It's easier to read – after all, newspapers, the world's best-read literature, use columns that are narrow in the extreme.

Condense copy. You'll need to keep within the space restriction. Don't say, on behalf of your client, 'I have had five technical papers published, the subjects of which were ...'. Say, instead, 'Author of 5 technical papers on ...'. Use contractions, such as 'inc.' for 'including' and '5' rather than 'five'. Keep sentences and paragraphs short, for easy reading.

Spell out achievements, not just responsibilities. Don't flannel or boast. My insurance collector client wanted to say he was a good mixer and listed 'socialising' as a hobby. An insurance salesman needs to be good company and personable, so this is not an irrelevant skill or attribute. But it needs to be quantified. For example, 'Helped host Premier Insurance hospitality tent at Epsom Downs trade fair. Contacted 213 invited and casual prospects, created record 57 new clients.'

Leave out trivia: weight, height, number of children, health, sex (unless client has a confusing name, such as Francis/Frances, Lesley/Leslie, etc.), marital status.

Avoid fancy presentation: folder, comb-binding, plastic jackets, tassle, exotic typefaces, excessive use of DTP (desktop publishing) and graphic techniques like newspaper style headings, photographs or images.

Take good aim before you fire off your clients' CVs. Don't assume they know how to address an employer or whom to target. Satisfied customers will come back for more. You'll also nurture business via the most powerful marketing technique of all: word-of-mouth recommendation.

Here's a rundown on the major CV formats. The **functional format** centres on abilities and work experience, grouped under key areas of activity. Angling for work training business clients in communications skills, I required a more focused CV. The name for this, in professional circles, is a **targeted CV**.

Nothing carries as much clout in the world of writing as a book published. So, my first sub-heading, under the block heading, MAJOR ACHIEVEMENTS, is

Author of 6 books

The Americans work also with **resumé alternatives**, which may be in the form of a longish personal letter, with attributes, skills, qualities, work or project achievements, listed in bullet point form. You can use blobs, asterisks, dashes or double dashes, and numbers. Anything that helps make the information more digestible, is good news.

HELPFUL READING

Resumés that Get Jobs, Edward C. Gruber, Arco Publishing Company (USA), 1965.

The Perfect CV, Tom Jackson, Piatkus, 1991.

GENERAL

Astrologer/Tarot Card Reader

1 FILE NOTES

Background and concept

Astrology and astronomy were one and the same study, until the seventeenth century. According to The Astrology Study Centre (see below), this larger study covers 'the whole of mankind's knowledge and beliefs about the heavens and the way in which these relate to every aspect of art, science, philosophy and religion.'

Today, astrology (as also Tarot card readings) is accepted as one of a number of divination systems, along with the less well-known I Ching and Runes. Modern-day astrologers shun the Gipsy Rose Lee image, and see themselves instead as professionals operating within the new and growing self-fulfilment industry.

Fortune telling doesn't come into it, according to a successful local astrologer Jane Sunderland: 'The planetary positions, according to a person's date, time and place of birth, shape character. And character is destiny. I don't predict precise future events so much as signpost forthcoming trends, good and bad, and suggest ways to triumph or cope with adversity, given individual strengths and weaknesses.

'A birth chart reflects You, your talents, inner conflicts, the pattern your life is likely to take.' The challenge for the astrologer is to enable clients to build on the predispositions in their characters.

'Once you become aware of who you are, you can take control of the pattern. Many people want to live a more creative life. An astrologer can reveal how to channel energies and achieve this end, living a life which is true to themselves and in harmony with the times they find themselves in.'

Is this business right for you?

Obviously you need to be a 'believer' in star signs, birth charts, the ability of the stars and planets to influence events and shape personality. Unusual sensitivity, empathy, and a naturally caring and curious nature will probably have made you a discreet and trusted confidante to friends, for whom you may already have drawn up well-received horoscopes.

Astrology is quite a study, as you will read. The ability to communicate your knowledge and theories and relate to clients must also rate high.

2 DOING THE BUSINESS

There is no officially prescribed route to professionalism. But there may be one day, if the European powers that be have their way. As it is, the training, whether formal or through independent study, can be quite lengthy and demanding.

Royal astrologer Penny Thornton, erstwhile consultant to the Princess of Wales, had what she describes as a 'classical training' involving four years of study with the Faculty of Astrological Studies, leading to its diploma award. 'It was a thorough ... training in astronomy, history and astrological theories and techniques, as demanding ... as any university degree course.'

Other astrologers are self-taught. Inspired by an 1890 book, *How To Cast Your Local Horoscope*, picked up in a jumble sale, Jane enrolled at an evening class in the subject and went on to become a member of The Association of Professional Astrologers by successfully submitting a thesis on *Pluto: Planet of Death and Transformation*. The membership door also opens to those who come with high personal recommendation, and to candidates who successfully complete the Association's diploma.

The astrologer typically reports on significant movement and change in a horoscope, helping clients recognise patterns in their lives and alerting them to changing 'winds and tides' in these patterns. Jane explains: 'These "wobbles" aren't necessarily specific. For example, if Uranus is crossing the base point of my horoscope, which corresponds to home and family, this could mean my daughter is going to crack up ... or the house is going to subside ... or my partner is going to suffer a crisis of confidence ... or I'm going to move house ... All we can do in such situations is alert people to shocks, breaks, disturbances and emotional and physical turmoil and suggest ways in which they could adapt and cope.'

An astrologer can get very close to guarded and intimate secrets, and needs to tiptoe around the sensitivities of clients. Not surprisingly, some astrologers find counselling courses useful, also helping them to improve their relational techniques.

Astrologers earn income via a number of activities: personal consultations, lecturing, broadcasting (TV and radio), telephone advice (live or pre-recorded), journalism (as a star-sign columnist). Clubs and societies, such as the Women's Institutes, are always looking for speakers and may pay a fee and mileage. Creating a high personal profile can lead to introductions to private clients.

The Association's recommended rates, as I write, are £45 to £75 per session. Jane charges £30 for a private consultation that may last up to an hour and a half. She doubts that her local market – or any provincial clientele – will stomach the higher rate, though Londoners may have the wherewithal as well as the commitment.

3 How to Market Your Service

Yellow Pages work for this, as for many other service-based businesses. But far better is word of mouth recommendation and getting known as a willing expert able to comment on astrological topics and advise newspaper readers, radio listeners or TV viewers on their problems and anxieties.

Jane was one of a team of resident astrologers working for a pub expensively and stylishly themed with astrological signs and symbols, and with its own consultation room and 'Astrology Computer'. When the pub felt the need to promote its benefits as an astrological forum, and pull in more clients (and drinkers), a PR expert was commissioned to get a local paper to use Jane to contribute a regular horoscope column. The column was sponsored, i.e., free to the paper, and carried the name, address and phone number of the pub.

Helpful Reading

The Forces of Destiny, Penny Thornton, Weidenfeld, 1990.
Romancing the Stars, Penny Thornton, Thorsons, 1988.

Useful Addresses

The Astrology Study Centre/The Astrological Association, 396 Caledonian Road, London N1 1DN (Tel. 071-700 3746).

The Association of Professional Astrologers, 22 Ruth Close, Cove, Farnborough, Hants GU14 9UX (Tel. 0252 520637).

The Faculty of Astrological Studies, BCM Box 7470, London WC1N 3XX (Tel. 071-700 3556).

═══════════════ ◇ ═══════════════

Minicab Driver

1 FILE NOTES

Background and concept

Drivers of London's famous black cabs (not always painted black!) spend time, sometimes years, 'on the knowledge', learning the geography of the capital so they can ferry passengers about efficiently and economically. They are licensed by the Metropolitan Police and strictly monitored.

Black cabs can ply for trade – in other words, you can hail one in the street. These licensed 'Hackney carriages' can also normally be hailed or approached at railway stations, airports, etc., in the provinces.

In London's suburbs, where black cabs are less in evidence, the provinces and rural areas, minicab firms proliferate and, sometimes, thrive. Minicabs are not legally allowed to ply for trade, though some risk prosecution and do. London minicabs do not (yet) need a licence; those working elsewhere are classed as Licensed Private Hire.

The heart of the bona fide minicab business is a telephone service and receptionist (male or female). Customers phone in their requests for a minicab and a cab is then dispatched to take them to their destinations.

Some cab drivers' cars are fitted with two-way short-wave radios, so the driver can be summoned and directed over the air. Others phone in for work, or simply return to base after each trip to await the next assignment.

Clearly, working without a radio link is hugely inefficient (as well as less safe), but it may be the only way to start, to get your foot in the door, prove your worth, with good time-keeping, courteous service, reliable car, and so on, before qualifying for issue of a coveted radio.

Some minicab firms have a proper high street, or back street, reception area, where people wanting a cab walk in off the street and wait their turn.

For reasons that have never been fully explained, the privately-run motor trade has an affinity for ageing khaki-coloured filing cabinets, upholstery that is high in calories, low in springing, and an atmosphere in which a non-smoker could learn to smoke without ever lighting up.

In an attempt to overcome this unappetising, macho image, a group of friends in London established a minicab service run and staffed by women. They were a hardy crew, and needed to be, given the traditional bloodymindedness, or even thuggery, of late-night customers, not to mention some of the trade's forceful ways with unwelcome competition.

Is this business right for you?

If you can handle this type of work there is, in its favour, total round-the-clock flexibility and rare cash advantages.

You'll need a full, clean licence, no drink driving convictions, a reliable car, a phone, a thick skin, a portable car vacuum and a supply of upholstery cleaner. You should have a thorough knowledge of the area you intend to cover.

2 DOING THE BUSINESS

You'll need 'hire and reward' insurance, which doesn't come cheap, and the right sort of vehicle.

Ideally, you want a four-door estate car with a diesel engine. Owning an estate car means you get first choice for long-haul airport work, where plenty of luggage is expected.

Volvo, Peugeot, Mercedes, Renault and Toyota offer estates with three rows of seats, effectively seven-seaters.

Minicab drivers charge in mysterious ways. Sometimes it's based on mileage, sometimes on the trip – in London there will be a stock charge to go to Heathrow or Gatwick airports, or the major railway stations. Occasionally it will be related to time of day – charges often rise by at least 15 per cent after midnight – inconvenience of the location, whether or not clients are expected to be drunk and so on.

A trip to an out-of-the-way destination, with a slim chance of a return fare, is another reason to rake up the cost; and of course your fare must take into account your return to base or home, or on to the next customer.

The minicab firm which 'runs' you may charge, say, 27 per cent of your takings for the benefit of their radio service, introduction of clients, advertising, premises and so on. Or they may levy a flat weekly fee for these services or charge a leasing fee for use of the two-way radio.

3 HOW TO MARKET YOUR SERVICE

If you are considering starting your own minicab service, talk to your local constabulary and discover the local view.

Running a cab office from home may be possible (with planning permission), or it may well create havoc with neighbours, given the extra traffic, occasionally unruly clientele and so on.

Minicab services rely on *Yellow Pages* and local newspaper advertising. If you did nothing more than distribute business cards through every door in your area, you would probably accumulate clients, long term.

Think laterally and devise some 'vehicle' for your advertisement that has eye appeal, high profile or built-in longevity. Consider advertising your phone number on tea towels, phone pads or some novel method of sticking your card to a phone.

Dog/Cat Hotel

1 FILE NOTES

Background and concept

The mainstay of this business is looking after dogs and/or cats while their owners are away. But it's easy to see how this activity can be combined with minding or breeding pets, walking dogs, grooming and even training them.

Is this business right for you?

Only committed pet lovers need apply. Your charges need to be fed, watered and exercised (dogs twice a day), and, on occasion, watched over as much or more than any sick child.

You should be a pet owner with many years' experience and enough knowledge to spot an ailing pet, which you may refuse to board (likewise unneutered toms and even puppies, both rejected as a matter of policy by some cattery and kennel operators), or to spot one that falls sick during its stay.

Ideally, you'll own a substantial, preferably detached property – homesick dogs are notoriously noisy – on which you can build proper kennels and create a good long run, which will save you the trouble, and danger, of walking the dogs in the street or along country lanes.

Owners, you will discover, are as fussy for their pets as they would be for their children over the environment, proposed menu and provisions for healthcare and proper maintenance.

2 DOING THE BUSINESS

Never mind the neighbours, who may well kick up a stink over your animal activities, you will need to apply to your local council for a licence under the Animal Boarding Establishment Act 1963, and also the planning department, who, like the environmental health officer, will want to visit and see what facilities you can provide, the scale, hygienic specification – heat, light, water supply, fire precautions, provisions for cleaning out and disposal of muck – and so on.

You'll need to establish a 'sick bay' and keep records of pet's arrivals and departures, which the local authority or an officially appointed vet can inspect at the drop of a Bonio.

With vets charging roughly as much as a private dentist these days, it makes sound fiscal and political sense to befriend a local practitioner. A vet can advise on layout and care generally; meanwhile, you can make a sensible financial arrangement over call-outs and treatment.

Not only will the vet appreciate this professional and businesslike courtesy, but you may well find the contact leads to a useful mutual marketing back-scratching exercise: a vet is in a very good position to put business your way.

You'll need wide-ranging insurance cover (try Pet Plan Ltd, see below) and a good legal eye cast over the contract you should insist the owners of your pet boarders must sign. This will cover possible accidental injury to pet, person or property; death of the animal; veterinary fees, etc.

Sick animals will absorb enormous amounts of your time, and certain types of pet, notably large active dogs, will make huge demands on your food reserves: be sure these factors are equitably built into your contract and fees.

Another good idea is a printed questionnaire to cover all the important points that can so easily be overlooked when owners are anxious to get away on their travels.

Even better is to send the questionnaire in advance, so the owner can use it as a checklist, to ensure you have a proper record of the pet's innoculations, special diet, that they bring with them favourite toys, brush and comb, note down the animal's name, recognised commands and so on.

3 HOW TO MARKET YOUR SERVICE

You need to reach local, preferably well-heeled pet owners. Advertise in parish magazines and local newspapers in the leisure section or the pets classified department. Leaflet insertion ensures very high profile and the leaflet is far more likely to be kept when the newspaper is jettisoned.

Remember: people are lazy. They may mean to cut your ad out but never get round to it. The leaflet neatly overcomes this dilemma. You should also proposition vets and pet shops to distribute your business cards or publicity leaflets.

HELPFUL READING

Kennel and Cattery Management (monthly journal), P O Box 193, Dorking, Surrey RH5 5YF (Tel. 0306 712712).

Kennel Gazette (monthly journal), The Kennel Club, 1–5 Clarges Street, London W1Y 8AB (Tel. 071-493 6651).

USEFUL ADDRESSES

Pet Trade and Industry Association, Bedford Business Centre, 170 Mile Road, Bedford MK42 9TW (Tel. 0234 273933).

The Kennel Club (address above).

Pet Plan Ltd, 10–13 Heathfield Terrace, London W4 4JE (Tel. 081-995 1414).

---◇---

Bed and Breakfast

---

1 FILE NOTES

Background and concept

Hiring out spare rooms in your house to short-stay guests tempts many people, especially those living in or near a holiday resort or tourist attraction, or in the centre of a busy town frequented by commercial visitors.

The bed and breakfast landlady or landlord can probably offer a warmer, more personal welcome, homelier facilities and a fresher, more generous size of breakfast for a half or a third of the lowest hotel tariff – and still come away with an acceptable income.

Is this business right for you?

They say one of the main heartaches with this type of business is the loss of privacy experienced; suddenly your home isn't entirely your own. Even if you are lucky enough to have a house where the guests do not invade your own or your family's living space, they are probably using your front door, hall and have first call on your time, if an early breakfast is booked.

They are certainly inescapably there in the territorial sense, something that can be particularly distressing for children and teenagers. Even pointing out the benefits of extra income to youngsters – the new affordability of ballet or horse-riding lessons, new clothes or toys – may not do the trick. Therefore the notion of doing b&b needs to be aired and shared with all members of the family first.

2 DOING THE BUSINESS

As with most business activities, there are rules and regulations, some sensible, some intrusive, most unavoidable.

For example, the sign you erect will need to fall in line with council planning department regulations for size and positioning; while the question of whether or not to have a VACANCIES sign showing is a moot point of strategy.

Look at it like this, if you do not have a VACANCIES sign up it's easy to turn away a b&b prospect you don't like the look of, on the grounds that you have no rooms available. But it's rather more embarrassing and awkward if your window sign is trumpeting that you have rooms free.

If you are in a holiday or touristy area your regional tourist office has a vested interest in seeing your business up and running successfully; apply at your Citizens' Advice Bureau, civic centre, town hall or local library for their address. There may even be an organisation run by and for b&b, guest house and hotel owners in your area.

Other authorities and bodies to be approached include your local environmental health officer, the fire prevention officer, rating authority (your rates may be raised if the status of the property is changed to 'business use'), planning department, if you are considering improvements to your accommodation (even putting a wash handbasin in a bedroom needs planning consent), insurance broker (for public liability cover and also to arrange business use protection).

If you are considering buying a property specifically for b&b purposes, make sure you get planning permission for any conversion work. Look closely at the small print of your mortgage agreement; it may preclude business use of the premises. You may be able to get financial grant help or loans from tourist and regional development bodies.

Whether buying new or adapting your present home, consider guest parking. Is there room enough in front of your property, or near by, for your guests to park without upsetting neighbours?

How you actually run your business, on a day-to-day basis, is something you can please yourself about – provided you also please your guests. Since the cost and hassle of laundering is one of the main drawbacks to this business, and you need to change linen and towels for each new arrival, it clearly pays to encourage guests to stay on rather than have a succession of newcomers.

3 How to Market Your Service

Registering with your local tourist authority, and conforming to their b&b guidelines (possibly right down to the number of coathangers needed per person!), may entitle you to a useful listing in the leaflets and booklets that are distributed free to tourists and visitors.

You can also advertise in the classified sections of Sunday and weekend newspapers, something which is particularly effective in the post-Christmas period when people find planning holidays a cheering exercise at a dull time of the year.

Don't try to paint a word picture in your small ad; instead get readers to send for your 'FREE leaflet and guide to the delights of . . . [your area]'. Ask your local tourist board for a selection of 'guide to the area' leaflets you can include in your own mailings.

If your house has charming features, show them, in a drawing or photograph. If the main selling point is a thatched roof, let that be your cover illustration. If the garden is stunning, show that. If the house is unexciting, include a postcard of the seafront or a local beauty spot. Postcard inserts cost you pence, yet were taken by professional photographers.

Your room charges can be arrived at through a judicious recce of the competition. People love bargains and 'special offers'. Drop your room rates for two or three-day breaks or accommodate children under five free, children under ten at half price.

HELPFUL READING

Bed and Breakfast Guide, The Ramblers Association, 1–5 Wandsworth Road, London SW8 2XX (Tel. 071-582 6878).

Britain Bed & Breakfast, edited by Tim Stillwell, Stillwell Publishing, 1994.

Doing Bed and Breakfast, Audrey Vellacott and Liz Christmas, David & Charles, 1982.

Catering

1 FILE NOTES

Background and concept

There are many ways to cater profitably from home. You can help private people entertain guests to dinner in their homes, doing at least part of the food preparation in your own kitchen; offer on-site private or commercial catering for indoor or alfresco events – garden parties, weddings, birthdays, anniversaries, fork suppers, hospitality entertainment; cook executive lunches or deliver ready-prepared food (or just interesting sandwiches) for office staff.

Is this business right for you?

You don't need a degree in home economics, a Cordon Bleu diploma or the latest Aga to cater from home, though you need to have been awarded more than average marks for cuisine as far as family, friends and dinner guests are concerned.

You will need to be comfortably in control in the high-pressure hothouse of a kitchen and servery, and have a remarkable ability to improvise when things go awry, as they certainly will.

Professional catering is hard physical work; not only on account of the standing involved, but you'd be surprised how many miles are covered, criss-crossing a kitchen floor, serving up and clearing food, loading and unloading a vehicle four times (think about it) for every outside catering assignment.

And it is also hard mental work: monitoring every aspect of the operation, timing, being a super boss and host or hostess at the same time, takes its toll on the little grey cells. If you can imagine cooking Christmas dinner for a very large family at the drop of a party hat, you'll begin to appreciate the life you are considering leading ... Obviously you will need to own a car, ideally a van or shooting brake.

2 DOING THE BUSINESS

Rather than run the risk of being summarily shut down, talk first to your environmental health officer, who will be rightly concerned about cleanliness of the premises (any pets in the house?), food reheating and storage temperatures, water supply, wash facilities (do you wash clothes in the kitchen?), disposal of waste, hygienic handling of food, construction and maintenance of premises, etc. You'll need insurance to cover the possibility of being sued for making someone ill, or damaging people or premises in the course of your work.

Start small, and expand as you need to, is the best advice for almost every business, and certainly applies to catering. Longer term, and depending on the branch of catering you opt for, you may need to purchase a second oven, install a back-up hob or cooker, a large console refrigerator, chest freezer, and invest in a large supply of (preferably matching) cutlery, crockery and glasses.

Eventually, you may need to invest in special catering cabinets that keep food warm, cool boxes, portable Butane cookers, and other sophisticated equipment that will enable you to produce that 'fresh from the oven' look and taste wherever your work may take you.

You'll need to locate a reliable source for bulk purchase of flour, sugar, eggs, dried fruit, fat, cooking oil, tea, coffee, alcohol, clingfilm, foil, paper plates and cups. Buying huge catering packs of food is only an economy if you don't throw vast amounts away because the unused food has gone off.

If you get involved in corporate hospitality the best charging policy is to levy an hourly rate for staff, mileage for getting to and from the venue, and double the net cost of the raw materials.

It's not so much what you offer, which must be fresh, appetising and so on, but more how it is presented – what professional touches you can add. For example, add nutmeg to mashed potato, a twist of lemon to mousse, Worcester Sauce and butter to warmed baked beans (served cold).

Male business eaters, contrary to popular belief, do not favour toad-in-the-hole and treacle tart for lunch. They tend to be figure-conscious, at least in public, and welcome tasty food that can be simply eaten, perhaps with fingers. French bread is easier to cope with than potato salad, and does double duty as an accompaniment to the cheese course.

3 How to Market Your Service

Try a direct mailshot, straight to the managing directors of companies *by name*. If you can make their mouths water – with a choice of half a dozen varied menus? – you will be in with a chance. Mention also that you are able to accommodate special diets (ethnic, medical), supply wine etc.

If your publicity material includes colour pictures of food (not as expensive as it sounds), remember to show cooked meals in giant close-up, rather than a picture of a chef or cook surrounded by a mass of raw food.

The usual advertising routes are open to you – window cards, newspapers. But the best response is likely to come from a local newspaper editorial feature on your catering service, preferably of the unpaid for, non-advertorial sort. Weave in some glowing praise from well-known local business figures who have become satisfied clients.

Helpful Reading

Catering from Home, Christine Brady, Pelham Books, 1980.

Mary Berry's Buffets, Mary Berry, Piatkus Books, 1986.

Cake Maker

1 FILE NOTES

Background and concept

Home-made cakes, light and fluffy, pillow-plump with cream, or richly moist and studded with fruit, are somehow the last word in home cooking. If your cakes are consistently successful there's a ready market selling them via health food stores, delicatessens, market stalls (including Women's Institute co-operative markets), and in the 'baked to measure' wedding, birthday and general anniversary and celebratory business.

Is this business right for you?

Family cake making is often a celebration of mood, a gesture of love on a plate; making cakes for money demands impassive commitment, discipline and organisation – be prepared to stop enjoying baking, at least for a while, or until the cheques come in.

2 DOING THE BUSINESS

Since you are offering food for sale to the public, your local environmental health department will need to be informed. They have sway over the cleanliness of premises and equipment, the temperature of food, water supply and washing

228

facilities, waste disposal, whether pets have access to the food preparation area, whether the kitchen is used for domestic washing and so on.

The planning department should also be told and you could be asked to stump up a percentage of the business rate for using part of your property commercially. Technically speaking you must tell your mortgage provider (they can refuse permission) and you will need public liability insurance to cover you against possible claims by people who buy your cakes.

You'll need to locate sources of cheap or wholesale supply of basic ingredients, such as flour, cooking fat and oil, dried fruit, sugar and so on – *The Grocer* magazine is a good source of supplier contacts. Wedding cakes are by far the most lucrative aspect of cake making. One cake maker I know pitches her three-tier wedding cakes at a reasonable price and still manages to incorporate the little personal touches that wedding cake customers insist on and appreciate.

This part-time cake maker notes the cost of her ingredients then doubles it to arrive at the charging price. Since one cake demanded 400 sugar roses, the fruit of 10 hours' labour, you can appreciate that time should be costed in.

My cake correspondent confesses to being fairly hopeless as an artist, but turns into something of a 'Constable in the kitchen' once she gets an icing tube in her hand. She uses pictures from magazines and birthday cards as reference material. She draws with an icing pen, rather like a felt tip but using edible colouring to sketch on the icing.

People don't always know what they want (or can realistically commission), and your quick inspiration may save a lot of time and trouble. My friend's birthday cake depictions include an iced horse's head for a horsey 18-year-old's birthday, Ariel (from Disney's *Little Mermaid*), Thomas the Tank Engine, elephants and frogs.

A client's request for 40 nudes and a Satyr atop her husband's fortieth birthday cake needed to be toned down somewhat: he had to make do with a sated Satyr and iced pin-ups wearing bright bikinis!

The trend is to lighter baking, with the top two layers of a wedding cake made of sponge and only the first layer of traditional heavy fruit. The sponge innovation requires a snappier preparation technique: fruit cake is long lived, but sponge cake 'dies' after a day or two. The marzipan, icing and decoration need to be quickly completed.

You can make your own fondant icing, using liquid glucose, egg white and icing sugar, though packet icing is much improved, with Renshaw's Regal Icing recommended for quick results. One home baker uses tragacanth to strengthen the icing, while elaborate iced flowers, with that delicate porcelain look, are wired out, using florists' wire and extra tragacanth to make a hard icing paste.

A useful and companionable introduction to icing technique is to join an evening class in sugar craft, or flower craft, as it is sometimes known.

3 HOW TO MARKET YOUR SERVICE

Presentation is a big stepping stone to success – remember always to include a printed tag bearing your name, address and phone number for reorders or further commissions. Keep a snapshot album of your cakes.

Shop window cards are an ideal low-cost advertising medium and again show what you can do with a crisp colour mini-snap of an unusual cake or two.

HELPFUL READING

Cake Making and Decorating, Mary Ford, M. Ford Publications, 1992.

Decorative Sugar Flowers for Cakes, Mary Ford, M. Ford Publications, 1991.

Laundry Service – Washing, Ironing and Mending

1 FILE NOTES

Background and concept

Running a private laundry and valeting service – washing, ironing, mending and generally maintaining clothes – used to have a prescriptive addendum: '. . . for live-alone men'.

These days, it's a service that will sell equally well to working mums, women who hate domestic chores and don't give a fig who knows about it, and to the aged and/or infirm of both sexes, who are fed up with, or no longer able to handle, the drudgery of keeping clothes clean, and their wardrobe in a viable and economical state of repair.

The point is that you do a number of things for your clients better than laundries can – assuming there is a 'proper' laundry available locally to them, prepared to do an equivalent amount of cleaning and caring at any price.

For one thing, laundry equipment can be notoriously harsh on clothing. Also, delivery services are few and far between; surprising in what ought to be a growth industry, and another way in which you can score over the high street opposition.

And lastly, they charge prices that puts everyone except top executives back into the DIY laundry bracket.

231

Is this business right for you?

You need to be prepared materially, physically and mentally. Nobody who is regularly 'behind' with their own washing and ironing, or who finds this type of work tedious or demeaning should consider it.

Ideally, you should live in or near a town or city, own a large garden with a long clothes line or carousel. You enjoy wash day, are motivated by being 'on top of the job', thrill to the sight of a pile of neatly folded and buttoned shirts and blouses, and are a dab hand with a needle and cotton.

2 Doing the Business

You may need to beef up your own washing infrastructure. Consider buying an extra, second-hand top-loading twin-tub machine. They look ugly (like a chest freezer), require you to drag the sodden, clean washing across to the spinning 'hole', and generally keep on the ball for the whole of the wash cycle, whereas an automatic lets you watch TV or cook a meal. Not surprisingly, few people want them so there are little-used bargains to be had. For this type of work, however, they are hardy and ideal.

Pros don't use steam irons, by the way, they use cheap low-tech ones and work with plant spray bottles filled with ordinary tap water.

If you are handy with a needle and thread, and own a moderately good sewing machine, there are also good pickings to be had mending and altering garments (which, you should insist, must be clean), as a value-added valet service.

Good clothes cost a fortune, yet their death-rate is high. Many a male will hang up a pair of trousers for good once the bottoms fray. Yet they can be simply turned and lined with special cloth that absorbs wear so they will last a lifetime. The same applies to jacket cuffs.

Then there are alterations. People put on and lose weight; clothes which used to fit suddenly don't any more. Offer to let out or take in the waist-bands of trousers.

Offer to replace zips – a real bind when they go in trousers and skirts – and to reline pockets. Shirt collars can be turned, sleeves shortened and cuffs turned to hide fraying.

Hand finishing, allied to a cleaning and valeting service, is another smart idea. Get suits professionally dry cleaned first. It's the lining of jackets that is most often neglected. It must be pressed separately and carefully by hand. Lapels need to be rolled, not pressed flat. But the tell-tale sign of a top-class valet service lies in the pressing of pockets. Lift the flap on the pocket of a jacket. Nine times out of 10 you'll see a ridge where that flap has been pressed right into the cloth of the body of the garment.

3 HOW TO MARKET YOUR SERVICE

Advertise your service locally in shop windows. Get the friendly and personal element into your advertisement.

> I hand launder and mend shirts and blouses. Jackets and trousers altered. Linen service. Delivery and collection. Fast turnaround, low prices. Phone for details . . .

For washing and ironing, should you charge by the hour or per item? An hourly rate is generally favourable to fast workers, but does not inspire confidence in customers. Some won't trust your time-telling ability; others will be anxious about not knowing the bottom line before you start work.

Local newspapers are also a good bet. Shops not directly in competition – the haberdasher or general store that supplies you with cotton and thread – may take a window card.

Door-to-door leaflet dropping is another worthwhile idea. Target the estates, sheltered accommodation and student digs: not all students are either unkempt or broke.

Hairdressing

1 FILE NOTES

Background and concept

Most people relish their trip to the hairdresser, hair cutter, stylist or barber. Not only do women use their visit as an instant pick-me-up, men do, too, if the truth were told.

And, there is nothing like having your hair done in your own home or your hairdresser's home. Enjoying a good old chin-wag is an essential part of personal grooming, and the more private you are the livelier the wag.

Home hairdressing can also be the marketing focus for a variety of subsidiary services, such as beauty care, electrolysis, manicure, pedicure, massage and image consultancy, which can enhance earnings.

Is this business right for you?

Nobody should consider going into hairdressing without a professional qualification and adequate hands-on experience. The 'academic' side of training may take as long as three years and there is usually a two-year salon apprenticeship while 'improvers' learn the ropes.

Other than that, you will (ideally) have an outgoing personality, be chatty, interested in people, creative, up to date with the latest hair and fashion styles, fit enough to stand for long periods, have good colour eyesight and sound organisational skills.

2 Doing the Business

Hairdressing is one of the most versatile home businesses. You can see clients in your home. Travel to clients' homes. Or operate from home as an itinerant professional, working as casual help in a salon or, more illustriously, renting a chair in a salon and building your own clientele.

From talking to a number of self-employed, home-based freelancers, it's clear they have a problem making commercial sense of the non-productive time spent travelling to clients and the cost of petrol, for you need to be independently mobile.

Hairdressers rarely manage to sustain enough regular clients to generate the equivalent of a salon salary. Inevitably, and usually with regret, some home hairdressers drift back to a PAYE salon job. What goes wrong? The answer is faulty perception – and an inappropriate pricing policy. For the customer a prime benefit of having hair done at home is not having to travel to a salon. Transport costs money; even walking to a nearby salon costs money, in terms of time lost. Far from charging less than salons, as most home hairdressers do, they should charge as much or more.

Working from home, you need no special hair washing facilities, though a cable shower spray over the bath that can reach your sink is a good idea. You can cut clients' hair anywhere near a bathroom.

A console hood dryer on a stand is an occasional necessity, but most clients prefer their hair to be dried with a hand dryer. Some types of perm are easy to handle, but those demanding infra-red drying, and the more complicated solutions and appliances may be more difficult.

I know one home hairdresser who has landed a contract to work three mornings a week as 'resident' hairdresser to a local nursing home. The home funds basic shampoo and set fees, while the patients stump up the cost of perms, as needed. She trained for two years at college, gaining her City & Guilds and Northern Counties hairdressing certificates. She

235

says it's important for people to know you're associated with the Hairdressing Council. She pays an annual fee to register as a State Registered Hairdresser and append the letters SRH after her name; you can get special State Registered appointment cards.

Contact the authorities listed below or your local college for an up-to-the-minute list of courses.

You need to tackle the familiar hurdles, for a home-based business, of planning permission and possible rating reassessment. You will need proper insurance cover to protect you against customer claims, accidents on your premises, etc.

3 HOW TO MARKET YOUR SERVICE

Try shop window cards and local newspapers; a chemist shop where you buy your preparations might agree to display some of your cards. A leaflet drop around local streets is probably the best method of all. Offer to do mother (or father) and children at an all-in introductory rate.

The secret of enduring success in the home hairdressing business is to make the follow-up booking a natural part of your 'goodbye' routine. Miss out on this step and your clients will wander into the latest trendy high street salon, 'just for a change' or to 'see what they can do'.

HELPFUL READING

Hairdressers Journal International, Room H1521, Quadrant House, The Quadrant, Sutton, Surrey SM2 5AS (Tel. 081-652 3204).

State Registered Hairdresser (thrice yearly, published by the Hairdressing Council), 12 David House, 45 High Street, London SE25 6HJ (Tel. 081-771 6205).

USEFUL ADDRESSES

Hairdressing Training Board, Silver House, 17 Silver Street, Doncaster DN1 1HL (Tel. 0302 342837).

The National Hairdressers' Federation, 11 Goldington Road, Bedford MK40 3JY (Tel. 0234 360332).

Freelance Hairdressing and Beauty Federation, 16 Chancelot Terrace, Edinburgh EH6 4SS (Tel. 031-552 0732).

Dressmaker and Alterations Service

1 FILE NOTES

Background and concept

Bespoke dressmaking is a rewarding (in both senses) occupation that fits in well with family life. You may start by making up ready-cut shop-bought patterns, using customers' own material, and move on to making your own patterns.

Useful pin money will come from repairs and alterations, and the flow of 'lookers' should boost your fully-fledged dressmaking trade – keep samples of your work hanging on a rail, and also a scrapbook with colour photographs of clothes you've made and customers wearing them.

Is this business right for you?

Does your dressmaking skill make the grade? Can you follow and adapt a pattern? If your work is more stylishly cut and better finished than shop-bought fashions and if people compliment your own-made clothes, this could be the right home business for you. Of course you can study and improve your skill at an adult education centre or apply for one of the correspondence courses advertised in specialist and women's interest publications.

Are you reliable and disciplined enough to work to deadlines? Garments may be commissioned for special occasions. Miss the boat and you might just as well rip them up for dusters – along with your reputation!

Are you patient, flexible and understanding? You might want to create tomorrow's fashions, but often customers go to private dressmakers because they prefer yesterday's look.

You'll need a warm, presentable workroom where you can fit customers, and a convenient, private place for them to change, without them tripping over children's toys or having to walk through the lounge when *EastEnders* is on.

2 DOING THE BUSINESS

Your work/reception room must be well lit and big enough to hold an ironing board (which will be up all the time), steam iron, sleeve board, dressmaker's ham, long, tilting (cheval) mirror, a completely adjustable dummy bust, large cutting table and dress rail. You'll need a stock of picture-book styles, wads of cloth samples (easily obtained from cloth stockists) and a good versatile sewing machine, the best you can afford.

When buying your sewing machine choose a big store with a reputation to lose, in case things go wrong, or you need a bit of expert personal instruction. Get the demonstrator to show what the machine can do and be sure you are comfortable with the gadgetry.

If you plan on working with denim and heavy velvet, you'll need a heavy duty sewing machine. A standard attachment for zips and gathering is useful, as is a reverse stitch device.

Your charges will reflect the wealth or otherwise of your area, your skill and time, what others in the same line of business charge and so on. Whether you charge by the hour or per assignment (with materials and trim added on), remember to include payment for time-consuming trips to buy buttons and zips. Include one fitting in the basic price, but alert your customer to the possibility of additional cost if special items are needed or specified.

If you dread handling heavier clothes, refuse to do it. If a customer has hopeless taste let her down gently: 'I saw a model girl in a magazine wearing a dress in this fabric and it made her look frumpy ...'. Be bold and say it – or you'll be blamed when the customer looks a sight in the street!

Customers who pay over the odds to have clothes made to measure, for themselves, or their children, expect special treatment. Clothes (for anyone, of any age) should be judged by feel, weight, attention to detail in the parts that *aren't* on show. Children's clothes, with their regime of wear that wouldn't disgrace a rodeo-rider and near-on daily washing, need to be doubly durable.

One maker of children's clothes creates her own USP – unique selling proposition – by choosing only crisp 100 per cent cotton cloths and a distinctive but strictly limited range of patterns. Buyers go overboard for the luxury aspects – bodices and trousers are lined – and the flexibility, a customer selects any pattern made up in any stock material.

3 HOW TO MARKET YOUR SERVICE

As well as your work, the quality of your image counts too. Keep a smart-looking appointments book, and order some decent business cards, receipts and stationery. You'll also want to specify some distinctive sew-in tags, bearing your name or logo, to sew in the backs of your garments.

Advertise locally for business – window cards, newspaper, parish magazine, pinboards where mothers congregate (crèches, nurseries and so on). As you build your business work will come in from personal recommendation. Impress your returning customers by keeping a record of their unvarying measurements like nape of the neck to the waist and underarm, though of course you'll have to check hip, bust and waist for every new commission!

Antiques Restoration

1 FILE NOTES

Background and concept

If buying and selling antiques is no longer (was it ever?) a passport to easy money and a freewheeling lifestyle, restoring them remains one of the more reliable ways to make money.

Basically, there are three main types of antique which lend themselves to home repair: wooden furniture (not necessarily small); porcelain and pottery; and upholstery pieces.

Who pays for restoration work? Dealers do. They hoard old broken items in the hope that some day there will be the time or opportunity to get them fixed and realise the profit that is trapped in the stored shards and splinters. A competent, confident restorer, could make their dreams come true rather sooner.

Collectors are another source of income. Collectors will pay more, because amateurs expect to; but they will give you a harder time over timing and be fussier, and, obviously, the turnover of antiques in the private sector cannot equal that among professional traders.

As well as repairing antiques for other people, you can invest in your own cheaply bought antique version of what the motor trade calls 'damaged repairables' and do them up to be sold at a profit.

Is this business right for you?

You could be a gifted teenager or a disabled pensioner and still make a go of restoration. Common sense, good eyes and steady hands are all that's needed. One pro restorer says anyone with 'craft aptitude' can get started in a home repair business after 10 to 20 hours; folk with more thumbs than two will need 30 to 40 hours of study and application.

This expert was talking specifically about 'shoebox antiques' – ivory and porcelain figures, tea cups, snuff boxes and decorative ceramics. The cruder forms of woodwork repair are well within the reach of any competent DIY person.

2 DOING THE BUSINESS

Strictly speaking, this section is about repair as much as restoration. A restored antique has pieces missing which need to be replaced and possibly manufactured, by you, from scratch.

Cracked or broken items, with all broken pieces recovered, can be repaired. Inevitably, every break involves some loss of material, whether it be splinters of wood or a spray of porcelain dust.

What looks like a clean break in china, under a magnifying glass or microscope, never is. Only wood, ivory (except brittle old ivory) or plastic stand a chance of being repaired 'seamlessly', with little creative input from the restorer.

There isn't the space here to go deeply into restoration techniques. Suffice it to say that there are two main ways to fix broken antiques: by glueing surface to surface, simply; and by glueing with reinforcing pins, the latter being far more resilient.

The skills required to repair porcelain and pottery are akin to those of a laboratory technician making and repairing dentures. John Zionmor, whose book is mentioned below, in fact abandoned a burgeoning career as a dentist to take up the more lucrative occupation of antiques restoration!

Woodworking repairs are rather more accessible to anyone

with a good set of standard workshop tools and some specialist equipment that can be bought according to need.

Some of your best finds will be furniture that looks a lot worse than it is. It may be dirty with joints that have worked loose. Simply removing layers of old, tired polish will transform many pieces. Yet it's a curious fact that many antique dealers are not keen to get their hands dirty. Often they'll pass up a potential gem of a table or otherwise saleable set of chairs just because there are lame members in the family.

Cosmetic renovation – perhaps to a chest of drawers that has bubbled and bleached from being left too long in a sunny alcove – may also be within your scope. But because you are in business to make money, rather than restore to original condition, you must set your own purchasing cut-off point.

With a chest, for example, once the thing looks right, and the drawers run smoothly, you could sell and take your profit, and never mind that the back is plywood-patched.

It will pay you to understand the antique market. Keep your ear close to the ground, subscribe to *Antiques Trade Gazette*, watch what sells in antique fairs and stores. You'll discover, for example, that individual chairs, like the ubiquitous Victorian balloon-back, are often bargain priced when bought individually and slightly damaged, but treble in price when they come in a set of four or six.

Pine (especially eighteenth-century pine) is a perennial favourite. Early pine should be stripped by hand using Nitromors, but later, cruder items can be dipped in caustic soda, though you don't need to tackle this messy, dangerous job yourself: find a professional 'stripper' in *Yellow Pages* or *Antique Dealer and Collectors Guide*, or ask in your local stripped pine shop.

I spoke to Albert Jackson, co-presenter of the successful BBC television series *Better Than New* (book available, see below) about the business aspects of restoration. Buy at auction, he says, but don't sell there. Instead, use local newspapers and shop window cards. Or take a stand at a one-day craft or antiques fair. Try to build a file of customers looking for specific pieces. Then you can buy with a near guarantee of being able to sell on after restoration.

'You must allow for your time at a proper professional rate,' he insists. 'Some amateurs feel that if they buy for £50 and sell to a dealer for £70 they have taken a healthy profit. But they take no account of the hours of work they have put in.'

3 HOW TO MARKET YOUR SERVICE

As an absolute beginner you might have to buy some 'damaged repairable' item in an antique shop, take it home, restore it, and take it back for appraisal and hopeful sell-back – business cards are a must.

With luck, you'll be offered further commissions by a gleeful dealer. Restoration author John Zionmor found that on the strength of the reliable quality service he could offer, many dealers cheekily placed 'ANTIQUES RESTORED' cards in their windows!

All the familiar small-scale publicity routes are open to you: shop advertisements, newspaper classified advertising, leaflets inserted in the local newspaper (far more impact than even a large ad in the paper, if tastefully done).

HELPFUL READING

Antique Restoration Profits, John Zionmor, Chartsearch Limited, 1982.

Antiques Trade Gazette (weekly trade newspaper), available on subscription (UK, £40) from Metropress Ltd, 17 Whitcomb Street, London WC2H 7PL (Tel. 071-930 4957).

Better than New, A Practical Guide to Renovating Furniture, Albert Jackson and David Day, BBC, 1982.

Upholsterer/Rush and Cane Repairer

1 FILE NOTES

Background and concept

Upholstery is one of those DIY skills that commands unusual respect among friends and relatives (a great source of commissions), and offers the prospect of fairly serious rewards, especially when operated as a complete service, which may include the supply and fitting of curtains, loose covers etc.

Cane and rushwork – refurbishing the seats of chairs, the seats and sides of a bergère suite, and so on – are subsidiary activities you could profitably consider.

You can offer an upholstery service privately, to antique dealers; work as an out-worker for an established upholsterer; or use your eye for furniture with fine lines, to buy up cheap, neglected pieces, shabbily upholstered, at auction or in markets, and restore them to sell at a profit.

Is this business right for you?

Upholstery is one of the more robust crafts. You'll need a fair amount of physical strength, or a readily available friend or partner, to move the larger pieces around just to work on, never mind loading on to and unloading from your vehicle.

At home, expect to lose the use of at least one large room, for working in, and possibly even more space, set aside for storing fabrics, 'work in progress', tools and so on.

Hammering and machining, delivery and collection, may draw the attention of neighbours in a close community or estate situation. Be sure you aren't treading on too many toes; not least, those of the council planning department.

Training – there are many routes – is essential. You'll be dealing with expensive materials and valuable furniture; mistakes and accidents could be costly. Investigate public liability insurance, in case you 'damage' any people in the course of your work, and professional indemnity to cover damage to furniture and furnishings.

There are full-time upholstery courses, three-year apprenticeships and long-term adult education courses on offer. Aim, at least, for a City & Guilds or National Federation of Women's Institutes qualification.

2 DOING THE BUSINESS

You'll need to invest in a fair amount of equipment, including blunt-nose shears, Stanley knife, web stretcher, shears, needles, springs, frames, upholsterer's hammer, as well as 'consumables', such as canvas, webbing, horse hair, down, feathers, foam, flock, calico, wadding, linings, castors, adhesive, tacks etc., which will need to be billed to clients.

Most domestic sewing machines will not cope with the stouter forms of upholstery material, though fine for curtains and loose covers. Expect to buy a heavy duty workshop machine with a piping foot and able to take professional attachments.

You'll need to be *au fait* with the latest fabrics, the pros and cons of various synthetic materials. Also advisable is a skilled carpenter on hand who can repair the inevitable defects in frames, stretchers etc., that come to light once the cloth is stripped away.

Approach materials manufacturers for sample books to show customers. Be generous and willing when customers ask for a snippet of material, or braid samples to take home to match with existing furnishing or the paint colours and paper patterns of a planned redecoration scheme.

Accurate ordering of material is vital. Where possible, do the measuring yourself. If customers are taking measurements, make sure they know exactly how to do the job. Offer clearly printed or typed instructions, possibly with a sketch or diagrams to hammer home your written instructions.

Bear in mind the nap of cloth. It will need to run in a particular direction and this can make a dramatic difference to the amount of material you need to order.

Think small, to start with. This means keeping away from elaborate pieces like *chaises longue*, springing or buttoning, at least until you have a secure knowledge of your new craft.

If you take on curtain making, be prepared to do the whole job, which may cover measuring, help with selecting suitable material and trim, and hanging them for clients.

This is less of a bind than it might sound: if you can buy curtain poles, rails, rings, hooks etc., wholesale, there's extra money for you if you charge at the more familiar retail rate.

If you're good with your hands, consider restoring cane and rushwork. The seats of antique chairs are the most familiar candidates for repair, and cane has been used for cabinet doors, the tops of stools, bed-heads.

Canework, an ancient Chinese craft, goes back to the seventeenth century in Britain. Cane comes from the stem of the rattan, a palm from south-east Asia. The strips are pared from the glossy, hard surface below the bark.

There are two main methods of caning. Either the cane is woven (in one of two bold and pleasing patterns) across the opening (chair seat, bed-head etc.), inserted through the drilled holes and pegged. Or ready-made sheeting is used and glued in place, and beading applied to mask the seal.

This last method is not as strong as woven cane, but neither is the sheeting technique as modern a short-cut as it sounds: the Victorians used sheet cane, too.

Caning a chair in the hand-weaving technique takes about eight hours, and is commonly priced by the number of holes. Rushwork is priced by the size of the chair.

Cane needs to be damped before and during work; while rushwork calls for a large sink or bath to keep the rush, or cheaper seagrass, moist and pliable. To get started you need a good book (see below) and a few basic hand tools.

3 HOW TO MARKET YOUR SERVICE

Refurbished antique furniture, especially low-price, desirable small-scale items, such as prie-dieu, nursing chairs, footstools, odd chairs, ottomans and so on, are easy to sell via shop window cards, especially if accompanied by a colour snapshot of the piece, with size reference – a vase of flowers, newspaper, wine bottle, close by.

Consider also taking space at craft and antique fairs, or possibly renting space at a local antiques centre..

HELPFUL READING

Wicker, Cane and Willow, Beth Franks, Weidenfeld & Nicolson, 1990.

USEFUL ADDRESSES

Fred Aldous, The Handicraft Centre, PO Box 135, 37 Lever Street, Manchester 1 M60 1UX (Tel. 061-236 2477).

National Federation of Women's Institutes, 104 New Kings Road, London SW6 4LY (Tel. 071-371 9300).

Picture Framer

1 FILE NOTES

Background and concept

There's a lot more to picture framing than just slapping prints, paintings, photographs and needlework into a sandwich of glass and board, and trimming them with glass or wood strips. Your aim should be to undercut the high street 'fast framer' on price and overtake on quality. Both should be achievable.

Is this business right for you?

You must be good with your hands, accurate (mistakes are expensive in terms of wasted materials), painstaking, and with a good eye for colour and balance. The most sympathetic framers seem to have had some artistic or design training. The ability to select an optimum shade and width of mount, an appropriate frame, a knowledge of materials, paint, paper and fabric . . . these are not God-given skills.

There are also practical constraints, such as having room for a workshop, and a vehicle with adequate space for carrying home stock from suppliers and wholesalers.

2 DOING THE BUSINESS

According to *Picture Framing from Home* (see below), you can get started for very little. Having said that, you would need to acquire some fair amount of skill, and a heap more tools and equipment.

Conservative estimates put the workroom space needed for picture framing at about the size of a double garage. You will need this space not only for cutting and working on glass, mounts, framing wood and backing board, but also for storing the aforementioned, storing work in hand and also stacking work awaiting collection.

You'll need enough room to house the table tennis table area of flat space you will need to work on. A couple of stout old dining tables will do fine, even if it means covering them with hardboard to create a flat, flawless work surface.

Other essentials are a power source for electric tools, good electric lighting (quartz halogen is best, neon tubing is cheapest) and preferably also ample natural light.

Top quality picture framing gear is awesomely expensive: some thousands of pounds to buy new. You might find second-hand equipment offered by a privateer selling off unwanted equipment or a professional framer throwing in the towel, in *Exchange & Mart*, craft magazines, or local buy and sell publications, such as *LOOT*, in London.

Any old tools won't do in certain departments. You'll need the best mitre-making box you can find, the precision cut of a mitre being one of the acid tests of a good frame-maker; in addition to a glazier's gun, glass cutter, clamps to hold mitres being glued (for working in a traditional style with antique frames), vice, T-square, heavy steel rule, industrial size roll holder for brown paper that seals the backing board.

Improving or acquiring skill may mean following an intensive course at a local adult education class. Or find a residential course to suit, such as that at West Dean College, West Dean, near Chichester, Sussex (Tel. 0243 811301).

Maintaining adequate supplies can be a bind. Should you keep just a display of mitred corners in various moulding styles? Or should you keep proper lengths of moulding, to save the hassle of waiting for delivery or going to collect, or worse, risk the wholesaler being out of stock, when you phone through your departed customer's order? The dilemma is artistic as well as practical. A connoisseur client with a fine picture to be framed will insist on seeing a proper 'run' of framing. Don't forget that you will need proper professional insurance cover to protect against the theft of customers' pictures and possible accidents. You should also contact your planning department and mortgagor for permission and approval of your home framing activities.

On a more mundane note, you may need to come to a workmanlike understanding with your dustmen about disposal of glass offcuts, since removing these may be outside their usual remit.

3 HOW TO MARKET YOUR SERVICE

Make your service known to local arts and craft shops, art and photographic classes, advertising agencies, designers; photographers' studios might show samples of your work.

Chemist shops that process prints are a good bet for displaying point of sale business cards or some other advertising device. You could make the point, succinctly in print and with a well-executed example, that a good snapshot, framed, turns into a work of art and a joy for ever.

HELPFUL READING

Antique Picture Frame Guide, Richard A. Maryanski, Cedar Forest Co. (USA), 1973.

A Complete Introduction to the Art of Framing, Eamon Toscano, D. Evans, 1973.

Picture Framing from Home, Thorn Publishing, PO Box 58, Winsford CW7 2XB.

◇ Photographer

1 FILE NOTES

Background and concept

There was a time when photography, as a home-based profession, was in danger of being swamped. Major advances in technology such as affordable autofocus cameras, built-in zoom lenses, self-adjusting flash, even a bizarre sort of preflash designed to narrow the pupil and prevent 'red eye', auto load, auto film speed setting (DX coding), auto rewind and so on, threatened to make picture taking all but fail-safe and idiot-proof.

Somehow, though, with the death of the dream that you can take perfect pictures merely by buying the latest gadgetry, people have become more appreciative of the skills of the professional photographer. Studio portraiture is booming and professionals are discovering that the package – the misty view (traditionally glycerine on a plain filter), vignetting, the frame, the oval mount – is the money-maker. Take as many snapshots of the bairns or the bride, as you like, it's the professional's portrait that earns pride of place on the sideboard.

Is this business right for you?

You'll know if your photographs reveal talent; people whose opinion you respect will have told you so. The litmus test? Pictures by good photographers make you feel as though you've stepped into the frame: their sitters seem so much closer and more vivid than other people's.

If the subject is a child, they'll have made an effort to get down closer to that smaller world by squatting down, bringing the camera's lens on a level with the child's eyes. Good lenspeople have an easy manner and a natural ability to make people feel at home even in squirm-making situations.

Consistency is another sure sign of talent. Does this mean getting it right every time? Far from it. Pros use film like it's going out of fashion. To the working photographer film is about as important as paper to the writer: it's the artistic statement that counts, not the economy of the exercise. Rather, consistency is the result of a critical self-awareness, and the ability to edit, ruthlessly and creatively.

2 Doing the Business

You'll need the facility to turn a small room – preferably with running water, certainly with a light and mains electricity – into your darkroom. Colour transparencies, or slides, are still beyond the scope of most home processing, but turnaround time from a busy city colour laboratory is usually quite good enough for all but the most urgent press purposes.

A room that converts into a studio is a boon, though you can make do with long paper rolls suspended near the ceiling; the paper unfurls on to the floor, under the subjects to be photographed, to give you a plain, shadow-free background.

Casual help – even an intelligent, interested child – will make your life easier and more relaxed, and this will show in your work. A car is a must wherever you live.

Amateurs go overboard with their equipment and the ads encourage the myth of the professional strung about with expensive equipment.

Nevertheless, there are significant advantages in certain features. I found working with TTL – flash monitored through the lens – a godsend. It meant I could forget about calculations and concentrate on making my subjects respond.

Never underestimate the usefulness of props. I always carry a pair of brief white panties in my camera bag to make people smile! It's never failed yet. They're also handy for winding round the flash head, to soften the glare.

More important than the lenses you use is the ability to work in a larger format. Most SLR and compact cameras use 35 mm film. It's cheap to buy, easily handled and comes in quite long lengths, usually either 24 or 36 frames per roll. The medium format film size, 2 1/4 in square, typically fits cameras like the old fixed twin-lens Rolleiflex, the large format Pentax and Hasselblad.

Although the medium format negative doesn't look that large it is several times the area of a 35 mm negative. This means enlargements can be far more successful in terms of richness of colour, lack of grain and so on. In addition, it's far easier to edit contact strips made from 2 1/4 in film. You can see the good shots at a glance and spot faults without a magnifying glass.

Must you have a studio? According to a professional friend, 'It's fine taking a picture of a baby. You put the baby on the dining table and get the mum to stand behind with a cloth. Mostly you can't rely on the background in a stranger's home, and there's no way to put up your own.' Getting people to come to you is the essence of professionalism in this, as in many businesses, and of course it's far more time-efficient for you.

After years of establishment, my friend's client range is well spread and relatively recession-proof. Portraiture, especially of children, is a clear favourite, and there are PR and advertising contracts for a public utility, and enough wedding work to send himself and his wife off to different receptions every weekend!

Nothing is charged for portraiture; the money is made on the prints the satisfied customer orders. Using a quality Polaroid camera, useful small change is made taking mugshots for passports, bus passes and ID cards.

Professionalism is likely to be the key to future success. My photographer friend is a Licentiate of the Master Photographers Association and working towards a qualification from the British Institute of Professional Photographers.

3 HOW TO MARKET YOUR SERVICE

Put an ad in the announcements column of the local newspaper and cards in shop windows. Go out knocking door to door, offering to take photographs of the owners' attractive homes, gardens, pubs. Use leaflet advertising and personal visits, taking framed samples of your work with you – a big proportion of your profit will come from providing an attractive frame at a tidy mark-up.

Ask to put your business card in the window of children's clothes shops (for a small fee, get the manager to drop a card into every store bag customers take out), and on the noticeboards in crèches and nurseries.

To 'blanket' an area, have an A4 or A5 leaflet printed for insertion in every copy of the best-selling newspaper or best-distributed local freesheet.

HELPFUL READING

Better Black and White Darkroom Techniques, Bob Casagrande, Blandford, 1982.

Cash from your Camera, Louis Peek, Fountain Press, 1970.

How to Sell your Pictures at a Profit, E. Bennett and R. Maschke, PTN Publishing Corp. (USA), 1971.

Photographing for Publication, Norman Sanders, R. R. Bowker Company (USA), 1983.

Professional Photographer's Survival Guide, Charles E. Rotkin, Amphoto (USA), 1982.

Watch and Clock Repair

1 FILE NOTES
Background and concept

One thing is clear. The ability to repair clocks and watches has become a rare skill in a growth area. Very simply, the quartz revolution has meant that modern clocks and watches now have almost no moving parts. And never mind that they are cheaper, lighter and more accurate than ever – one prestige watchmaker promises its timepieces will be a maximum of four seconds out per year! – people are coming to appreciate the mechanical ingenuity of earlier timepieces.

Look in every serious Sunday newspaper and you will find advertisements by dealers and shops (Austin Kay in the Strand is one active advertiser) looking to buy Rolex, Bueche-Girod, Piaget, Jaeger-Le-Coultre, Le Breguet, Cartier, Longines and Omega, especially the mechanical ones, hand wound or automatic.

Wristwatches from the 1920s onwards are becoming increasingly collectable as stylish objects to display occasionally, in much the same way as classic cars are the thing to own as a mark of understated good taste; to tend, and garage, but rarely to put on the road.

Collectors' watches are not everyday watches. In truth, they are not for telling the time with at all, but rather for looking at, with satisfaction and admiration ...

Is this business right for you?

Clearly, this is not a business for the ham-fisted, nor for someone with no mechanical bent or failing eyesight. It's a big subject, but the basics are surprisingly straightforward.

2 DOING THE BUSINESS

Start by reading a volume like Foulsham's *Clock and Watch Repairing for Amateurs* (see below). You'll need good light, a 'dedicated' table and specialist tools, such as pliers, nippers, movement blower, various tweezers, eye-glass, double control eye-glass, blueing pan, watch and clock oil, pegwood, as well as a lathe, probably the most costly piece of equipment – see the 'Repairer's Kit' section in Foulsham's book.

If you prefer to 'test the water' and your aptitude, start with cleaning, regulating and minor adjustments. If you own an old clock that's stopped, begin with that. Or buy a cheap one that's lost the will to tick. The easiest type of clock to understand and work on has a pendulum and weight.

The weight keeps the clock in motion, while the pendulum controls the speed and thereby the accuracy. A spring clock works in a similar fashion to a pendulum clock, but electric clocks are a different 'species' altogether.

Turn the wheels of your broken clock a few times. Can you spot a wheel that isn't moving? Can you see some dirt that's blocking movement and can easily be picked out? The professional watch and clock repairer always makes an intelligent guess before dismantling the timepiece.

A good idea is to draw a diagram of the clock's mechanism as you take it to pieces. Letter or number the pieces on the diagram as you remove them. On each part you remove scratch a number or letter to correspond with the parts on your drawing. This will help you put the bits back together again. To make sure you don't lose parts put them in a saucer.

Start your professional career 'close to home', with the

faulty timepieces of friends and relatives. With confidence you can begin to take in the clocks of strangers. At that point you will need to be fully insured, so that if you make mistakes they need not be expensive ones.

Consider joining an evening class to deepen your knowledge, enrol at a college course, or follow the correspondence course run by the British Horological Institute. West Dean College in Sussex offers an advanced year-long course in antique clock repair.

3 HOW TO MARKET YOUR SERVICE

Offer your freelance repair services to local antique dealers directly, jewellers who do not carry out clock and watch repairs, and to the public via advertisements in local papers, shop windows and self-publicity leaflets inserted into your local newspapers.

Coverage by this last route can be remarkably thorough and cheap too: my rural area paper, covering about 7 villages and surrounding districts, takes 2,000 leaflets and 'stuffs' them in their weekly newspaper for £30.

HELPFUL READING

Clock and Watch Repairing for Amateurs, H. Benton, W. Foulsham & Co. Ltd, 1928.

USEFUL ADDRESSES

British Horological Institute, Upton Hall, Upton, Newark, Notts NG23 5TE (Tel. 0636 813795).

West Dean College, West Dean, near Chichester, West Sussex PO18 0QZ (Tel. 0243 811301).

Market/Boot Fair Trader

1 FILE NOTES

Background and concept

Some people make a career of being a market trader; others use the markets as a part-time route to a kind of Walter Mitty 'other life' that is as invigorating as it is tax-efficient.

I remember once being on the receiving end of a woe-is-me tirade from a cabbie in philosophical mode. If you looked deep, he said, you'd find cabbies had tried all sorts of businesses that hadn't quite worked out. On closer inspection, they had another thing in common: the inability to take orders from anyone. Being a market trader has something of that flavour to it – with the added impetus that women are welcome and can generally hold their own with the men.

You can be an instant success, depending on your lines, prices, cheery personality or even the weather – if you're selling umbrellas in a rainstorm. On the street, failure is bad luck for the day only, not a branding for life. Now, there is a new type of part-time marketeer option; the boot fair trader.

Once you've tasted that early Sunday morning adrenalin, as you load up the car and head for the parking lot or field or waste ground, and the junk-hungry dealers close in on you, rabid for the freshest goods in the fair – yours – and you relish that unfamiliar cash-in-hand sensation, the question frames itself: is there some way of doing this more often? Yes there is, and I'll tell you how. But first . . .

Is this business right for you?

Not everyone is cut out to be a market trader. If you are lazy, slow with mental arithmetic, suffer from the cold or a weak bladder; if carrying things is a problem, or you hate getting your hands dirty or raising your voice and making an exhibition of yourself, then you won't make it in a street market. But, if you enjoy meeting new faces, can chat easily about nothing in particular, know how to wheel, deal and sell, if people describe you as a 'grafter', consider yourself eligible.

2 DOING THE BUSINESS

Ideally you'll need a van or a pick-up truck (with tarpaulin) or a car with an enormous boot. Boot fair traders, ironically, do better with an estate or a hatchback.

The best way for a beginner to get started is as a 'casual' in a run-of-the-mill street market; getting a full-time position in a top market is not easy.

When is the best time to get started? In the post-Christmas period, known as the 'kipper' season, the market dies and business stinks. You won't make your fortune, but you will stand a good chance of capturing a regular vacant pitch, especially if you move from market to market, checking for openings as you go. When you approach a market organiser the key questions are:

1. Can I hire a pitch for a day?
2. How much will it cost?
3. Can I hire or must I bring a stall?
4. Are there rubbish removal charges?
5. Where shall I meet the officer who controls the market?
6. At what time?

There may be no need to come fully equipped with a proper stall. It is not unknown for marketeers to debut as a 'suitcase Johnnie', in which case all you need is your gear and a strong pair of lungs – but make sure you get a licence first (Avril Harper's *Make Money Market Trading*, see below, is a guide to the drill and includes a list of market organisers to contact).

What should you sell as a market trader? The trick is to get into a selling line that is under-subscribed in a market. One of the best is china seconds, easy to buy in Stoke, the centre of the pottery industry. Even top factories have their seconds, handsome wares, flawed only to expert eyes. Junk, bric-à-brac and antiques are always sure-fire winners on stalls, but junk does not always rate as bona fide stock for some council-run markets, where you are asked to state exactly what you intend to sell when you apply for a licence.

Wholesalers, gift merchants, auctions of surplus and bankrupt and ex-government stock are all sources of merchandise for the market trader; details can be found in the publications listed below. Clothes, especially good, clean, used baby clothes, sell well in street markets and boot fairs.

Boot fair bestsellers include household cast-offs, junk, books, silverware, costume jewellery, framed fashion prints, interesting ephemera (old postcards, football and theatre programmes, songsheets, etc.), top hats and bowlers.

Any kind of market trading demands intelligent preparation. To save unpacking time, invest in some stacking plastic trays such as those butchers and bakers use. Travel equipped with an awning or plastic sheeting in case of rain, tablecloth (looks classier than bare wood), glazed display unit for valuables, safety pins to attach small items to your tablecloth to thwart thieves, small change float.

3 HOW TO MARKET YOUR SERVICE

When you get the urge to stretch your legs, have a wander,

but don't leave the market. Here, under your very nose is your best 'school for success', and it's free. Watch what sells, how other traders chat and display their wares.

One antique dealer's technique is to get round the front of the stall and mingle with the crowd. Standing alongside a punter means less eye contact, which is less threatening and is more conducive to a successful outcome. It's also easier to be heard and do deals if you don't have to shout.

People love to haggle, but they prefer to know the starting point and you will sell more if everything is price-marked.

HELPFUL READING

Make Money Market Trading, Avril Harper, £7.50 post free from the author, Avallan, High Hesleden, Hartlepool, Cleveland TS27 4PZ.

Markets Yearbook, World's Fair Ltd, PO Box 57, Daltry Street, Oldham OL1 4BB (Tel. 061-624 3687).

USEFUL ADDRESSES

National Market Traders Federation, Hampton House, Hawshaw Lane, Hoyland, Barnsley, South Yorkshire S74 0HA (Tel. 0226 749021).

Countrywide Markets (market organisers), PO Box 253, Worcester WR4 9UJ (Tel. 0562 777130).

Jobbing/Landscape Gardener

1 FILE NOTES

Background and concept

A jobbing gardener can offer a seasonal pruning service, digging flower beds, cutting lawns and so on. Fruit trees, roses and most shrubs need attention in early spring and autumn. Clearing undergrowth and keeping a garden in trim is also within scope of the gifted green-fingered amateur.

Further up the scale there is ready work for anyone who can plan and lay out a garden – a landscape gardener can earn serious money at a professional hourly rate and enjoy a pleasant, healthy life into the bargain.

With a decent-sized garden plot of your own there's a lively subsidiary market selling produce such as flowers, herbs, fruit and vegetables.

Is this business right for you?

Your fingers not only need to be green, they need to be strong, too. The bigger your own garden, the better. You'll need outside storage space for tools, plants and growing areas.

A sturdy vehicle (van, estate, pick-up truck) is essential. A ramp makes it easier to load/unload a lawnmower (battery or motor powered for preference), wheelbarrow, rotavator.

2 DOING THE BUSINESS

Quality tools will repay purchase down the years, but you don't have to buy new. Tools are auctioned in job lots at house sales, and you can find them in the better junk markets, such as London's Kingsland Road and Camden Lock.

Buy boxes, pots, compost etc. from a wholesaler. Careful cultivation will mean bigger profits. One 35p packet of seeds gives scores of plants which you can sell at 50p each. Plants that produce their own seed will demolish even that small overhead.

Vigorous, vividly coloured plants – geraniums, nasturtiums, wallflowers – sell easily to fruit shops, garden centres, DIY and hardware stores and petrol stations. Herbs, which are expensive to buy dried, are especially welcome fresh. Vegetables, particularly unusual varieties, also sell easily.

One gardening go-getter grew courgettes in jiffy pots in her greenhouse. These went straight to the local DIY shop. Next day she'd call back to pick up cash or plants. Soon she'd expanded sufficiently to work with friends. From October they were growing lupins, polyanthus and wallflowers in boxes.

When the greenhouse was cleared of bedding plants, they launched into perennials, vegetables, herbs and house plants. Her advice is to plump for fast-growing varieties and spectacular things like cucumbers and passion flowers.

Your own garden can be used for growing, naturally, and unless you plough the whole plot up for cultivation, there is usually no need to tell your local authority. A greenhouse is a must in the fairly short term.

Having an allotment, now in big demand thanks to the modern preoccupation with 'organically grown' produce, will dramatically increase your output. Check with your town hall to see how long the waiting list is. Or perhaps your council runs a share-a-garden scheme: old folk will let you grow produce in their oversized garden in return for part of the proceeds and your keeping their garden in trim.

To gain entry into bigger league landscape gardening, apply at your local market garden, country estate or nursery for paid-for training. Formal qualifications run from a National Diploma to a four-year degree course. Reading University (Tel. 0734 875123) and Pershore College of Horticulture, Worcestershire (Tel. 0386 552443) specialise in gardening.

3 HOW TO MARKET YOUR SERVICE

Canvass locally for work and commissions, keeping your tools and equipment close by, ready to get stuck in at the drop of a boater. Use window cards to advertise. Type a bold heading and underline it with bright felt-tip pen:

GARDEN HELP OFFERED

Your garden cleared of weeds, pruning, lawn cutting – plants supplied cheap. Also window-boxes to measure, fitted and filled with your choice of plants. Ask about low-cost landscaping service. I work fast and efficiently and clear all rubbish. Competitive hourly rate. Phone . . .

Advertise in local papers, parish magazines and through distributed leaflets – under windscreen wipers in the car parks of gardening centres, if you have the nerve!

HELPFUL READING

Beautiful Backyards, Roddy Llewellyn, Ward Lock, 1985.

Gardening for Effect (symposium), QED, 1984.

Painter/Decorator/ Interior Designer

1 FILE NOTES

Background and concept

The aim is to beautify and restyle the interiors of homes, rather than dramatically alter them, building extensions or carrying out loft conversions, though this work can be tackled once you have reliable, trained people – builder, carpenter, electrician, plumber etc. – whose skills you can call on.

Most of the time, people are being asked to pay for your design flair, your knowledge of novel and fashionable fabrics, paints and wallpapers, your contacts with builders, decorators and suppliers, and your ability to take away the headaches of bargaining and dealing with tradespeople.

Is this business right for you?

You probably have well-developed visualisation skills and a quick pen; an art school, design or architectural background is likely, as might be experience in antiques, upholstery, restoration, fashion, textiles or design journalism.

Magazines with homes and furnishing departments employ what have come to be called 'stylists', people who can effect a

266

'makeover' on a room as easily and vividly as the fashion and beauty editor will dramatically change the look of a reader.

Expect to consult on occasion in your own home, which should, as far as is practicable, be a showcase for your skills and design inspiration.

2 DOING THE BUSINESS

Although you don't have to be able to lay a line of bricks or build in shelves, it will pay you to know how these things are properly done, so you know when they are being bodged or improperly charged. You will find adult education classes specifically designed to teach women how to lay bricks, and classes in many building and design associated areas.

However, the beauty of this job is that you don't have to get your hands dirty. Your strength is seeing what others cannot imagine; hacking off plaster, skirting boards and dado rails is something workpeople can be paid to do.

As an adviser you will be entitled to a consultancy fee. More lucratively, you will supply materials and furnishings, commission the contractors, and supervise and underwrite the quality of the work.

Ideally you will handle all purchases, charging your client a commission for your efforts. As an accredited professional, you may also receive a commission from the supplier, and still save your clients money, overall, on account of your ability to buy at wholesale prices.

Cashflow is critical in any business involving large sums of money. The simple rule is never to put your hand in your pocket on behalf of a client. Never run up bills on your own account expecting a client to reimburse you later. If you act as a bank to a client, pretty soon one of them will take an unauthorised overdraft, default and leave you holding the tab.

If you can get suppliers to agree to bill clients direct, having first agreed this with the client, then it is up to the suppliers to run whatever credit checks they deem necessary.

This relatively safe way of operating can still go wrong; a slow-paying client can sour your own relationship with the supplier. It is much better to work only within the limits of cash or the (cleared) cheque a client has placed in your hand.

Have you heard the expression, 'Once a builder, always a cowboy?' There is much work to be done before that hat fits nobody. Pre-empt your public's anxieties about fly-by-night operators and then be as good as your word. There is no advertisement like word of mouth recommendation.

Be especially careful with work that may involve planning consent or building regulations. A listed building, or one within a conservation area, can also demand special materials and official sanction before work proceeds.

3 HOW TO MARKET YOUR SERVICE

At a basic level you can promote your services via shop window cards which should be tastefully designed and professionally printed. As your card is your 'shop window' it will pay dividends to show more. You could include a miniature view of a number of interiors you have designed, rather like those seaside postcards with multi-views, only more tasteful.

Remember always to take before and after photographs of your work, and keep them in a smart album. Nothing is so convincing and reassuring to a client.

Once you have an attractive business card, talk to potential suppliers – haberdasher, carpet or fabrics shop, antiques emporium, paint shop – and encourage them to display your cards in a prominent place, or even insert them in bags.

HELPFUL READING

The Ideal Home Book of Interiors, Peter Douglas and Clive Helm, Blandford Press, 1982.

The Which? Book of Home Improvements and Extensions, Consumers' Association, Hodder & Stoughton, 1983.

Antiques by Mail Order

1 FILE NOTES

Background and concept

Trading in antiques and collectables is traditionally operated via 'static' business methods. The dealer, full or part-time, runs a shop or hires floor/wall space at an antiques centre and pays rental which may include heat, light, security, publicity, management services.

Running a shop, or renting space is an expensive business. Both are slow, time-consuming, potentially tedious and commercially uncertain passive methods of selling.

In the Seventies, shrewd organisers began to exploit the new-found popular awareness of antiques and their decorative and investment potential by establishing antiques fairs.

Standing at fairs solved the passing trade problem by making the trader the active party. But travelling itself has become prohibitively expensive (fuel, food, accommodation costs); and this too has depressed the trade, obscuring its vast, relatively undiscovered potential – as a mail order business.

Is this business right for you?

You are unlikely to be considering this kitchen table opportunity 'cold'. You may already be a collector and your collection will form the basis of your new mail order antiques business.

Remember: this isn't a 'dabblers' option. Much of your trading will be to knowledgeable enthusiasts, keen to add to or improve their own collections. You'll need to know the subject and the market at least as well as your clientele.

If you can't 'do deals', if bartering or haggling embarrass you, turn to another home business – this one isn't for you. In order to sell stock you first have to locate and buy it – at the right price. Which means one at which you take a worthwhile profit, given your acquisition, marketing and running costs, your income needs and expectations.

There is also a writing element involved: describing, cataloguing, letter writing and so on. No copywriting skill is necessary: properly described/illustrated items will sell themselves (if the price is right). Marketing background (or instinct), however, is a plus.

2 DOING THE BUSINESS

Mail order antiques (for obvious reasons) tend to be items that are compact, sturdy, flat or easily packed (though styroform packaging means even brittle items can be posted safely). Fabric or paper are ideal items: ephemera – cigarette cards/silks (issued also in cigarette packs), Victorian scraps, bookmarks, early advertising and promotional material – posters, manuals, sales brochures (in a myriad sub-sections: aeronautica, automobilia, shipping, sport, theatricalia) – scripophily (early share certificates and busted bonds), beer mats, comics, magazines, story papers, sheet music, old photographs, fans, stamps, postcards.

Larger metal items are also keenly traded; among them tinplate advertisements, coins, medals, writing implements, penknives, model cars, soldiers, beer cans. Bulkier items, too, have a lively mail order following. Consider: woodworking tools, fishing flies/reels, corkscrews. Corkscrews form part of the wider activity of wine drinking, which includes early wine bottles, coasters, wine bottle labels, decanters, and so on.

When considering your own direction, think broad. China is well collected, but 'Disney China' (spotted in a 'wanted' ad in an antiques trade paper) has a much wider potential market.

The newer an area of dealing, the easier it is to become an expert if you're prepared to do a little digging. If you know, for example, three patentees of corkscrews, the chances are you know three times as much as an antique dealer who happens to have one corkscrew among the bric-à-brac.

Where do you find inspiration for new mail order antiques? Buy *Millers Collectables Price Guide* every year; subscribe to *Antiques Trade Gazette* – small ads in a recent issue revealed: 'DOCTOR REQUIRES PRE-1920 MEDICAL ANTIQUES ... OLYMPIC GAMES MEMORABILIA WANTED ... OCEAN LINER MEMORABILIA ... VICTORIAN MARBLES ... LLANELLY POTTERY.'

The essence of collecting is 'trading up', improving the quality of an existing flawed item, adding a missing link, and so on, to boost the tone of the collection as a whole. To this end, collectors buy but they also swap, and so should you. Boot and jumble sales are great sources, as are country auctions.

Buying antiques is an active, time-consuming activity; there may be many wasted forays before a killing is made! Once people know you are in the market for specialist pieces they will bring them to you or to your attention. Professional dealers often build a network of 'runners' who are constantly on the lookout for their mentors and are paid for their tip-offs and trouble.

A recce of the competition (if any), 'comparison shopping', is vital in this, as in any business. Some understanding of traditional mail order pricing techniques is also helpful.

The easiest sales literature is a list: the name or classification of the item, brief description, indication of condition, price.

Collectors want information, facts, details, substantiated

theories, provenance (origin, pedigree), with documents, references, etc. A picture is worth a thousand words. At least illustrate your star objects.

Ask for payment with order. Send nothing until cheques have cleared. Offer a money back guarantee for goods returned in unmarked condition, asking the sender to return items only via a 'proof of postage' system, also recommending that they obtain insurance for their returns. This is a business with international potential.

3 HOW TO MARKET YOUR SERVICE

Pursue all the traditional marketing routes: classified advertising in trade and local papers ('OLD POSTCARDS, WAR SOUVENIRS, 1950s ROCK'N'ROLL RECORDS . . . WANTED, ANY QUANTITY, GOOD CASH PRICE PAID, I COLLECT FAST').

The key route to getting your literature in the hands of prime prospects is via the small ad that invites enquiries: 'DRINKIANA COLLECTABLES. SEND 50p AND LARGE S.A.E. FOR ILLUSTRATED LEAFLET'.

There are other ways. Fairs are excellent places to distribute leaflets. Remember to get organisers' permission first.

HELPFUL READING

Antiques Trade Gazette (weekly newspaper), 17 Whitcomb Street, London WC2H 7PL (Tel. 071-930 4957).

How to Make Money from Antiques, Mel Lewis, Blandford, 1981.

Miller's Collectables Price Guide (annual), Millers Publications.

Bookseller/Remainder Sales

1 FILE NOTES

Background and concept

We know books are saleable door to door. Ask *Encyclopaedia Britannica*. Can you make money operating at a rather less grandiose level? The answer is yes!

Best of all, behind the doors I suggest you try are plenty of salaried prospects, some of whom will enjoy the privilege of being able to use expense account cash to fund their purchases . . . I'm talking about shops and offices, business parks and trading estates.

Your books – paperbacks and hardbacks – will be remainder stock, purchased direct from publishers. Remainder books are those that have failed to sell, often titles that are still topical and in mint condition.

Is this business right for you?

A hard-nosed personality and the gift of the gab are the key attributes. Other than that, you need to be mobile and within reach of a good number of city centres or trading estates. Having parked, there's a lot of walking involved, some carrying and quite a lot of waiting around, as receptionists go off to fetch whoever it is you've targeted as your prime prospect.

2 DOING THE BUSINESS

You don't have to be an author. Many publishers have books they're keen to be shot of.

The asking price for remaindered stock (to an author) tends to be about a fifth of the retail price. This 20 per cent equates, roughly, to the cost of production. In other words, the publisher tries to recoup its original investment in print.

One publisher suggested I buy up the outstanding stock of a business book of mine that had been in print for nearly a decade.

I happened to mention this 'on the table' deal to my accountant, who replied 'Make them a silly offer.' 'How silly?' I asked. 'As silly as you like. You have nothing to lose. You'd be surprised how often these silly deals get taken up.'

With mail order the rule-of-thumb mark-up is six times the acquisition price. In other words if you think you can sell a book for £3 through the post you should have bought copies of that product, or book, for no more than 50p.

Using my mail order rule-of-thumb, that an item should be saleable for at least six times the purchase price, I figured I could sell paperbacks for £1 (or more) each. This led to a purchase price of just 14p per copy.

Over one summer I peddled my books round more than a dozen local business parks, and through the commercial centre of Norwich, selling them for £3 a copy, or over 2000 per cent profit. In the aftermath of my successful experience I discovered a number of things that make this an outstanding home-based opportunity for anyone, not just authors.

Many publishers have titles they cannot clear (find their phone number in *Writers' and Artists' Yearbook*). Yet they seem to hate remaindering books to cut-price booksellers who offer them for sale in their brash bargain bookstores. Perhaps this failure is too public for publishers to stomach ... it hurts their pride (can you imagine what it does to the authors?). In any case, this is why they may be more receptive to the quiet private deal you might suggest.

To make money at this game, you need a daily plan, a good local map, a car full of petrol, a bag full of sandwiches, a flask of cool drink, some baby wipes for your brow and hands, and a change of socks and shoes: this is tiring work and every little bit of relief helps.

3 HOW TO MARKET YOUR SERVICE

Target business parks, trading estates, office blocks or just busy high streets with lots of shopkeeper prospects.

1. Choose a round figure, coins rather than notes. No one minds parting with loose change. More recently I've sold books for £1 or £2, to give positive impetus to that 'Why not buy?' reflex.
2. In some of the offices I discovered that books are a regular inertia sale. Agents for book companies leave sample books, usually of the coffee table variety, behind and return to fulfil orders and pick up cash. You might copy that plan.
3. Dress smartly, it opens doors. I ignored the 'REPS BY APPOINTMENT ONLY' signs and pitched for business anyway. Ninety-nine per cent of the time, your visit is a break in the monotony for nine-to-five folk.
4. Try a number of opening lines and adapt them as you learn which ones fall on blasé ears, and which intrigue and sell.

HELPFUL READING

Writers' and Artists' Yearbook (annual), A. & C. Black.

Index

Index